ETHNOMETHODOLOGY

ALAIN COULON
University of Paris VIII

Translated from French by
Jacqueline Coulon and Jack Katz

Qualitative Research Methods
Volume 36

SAGE PUBLICATIONS
International Educational and Professional Publisher
Thousand Oaks   London   New Delhi

Copyright © 1995 by Presses Universitaires de France
12, rue Jean-de-Beauvais, 75005 Paris

For information address:

SAGE Publications, Inc.
2455 Teller Road
Thousand Oaks, California 91320

SAGE Publications Ltd.
6 Bonhill Street
London EC2A 4PU
United Kingdom

SAGE Publications India Pvt. Ltd.
M-32 Market
Greater Kailash I
New Delhi 110 048 India

Printed in the United States of America

Library of Congress Cataloging-in-Publication Data

Coulon, Alain, 1947–
    [Ethnométhodologie. English]
    Ethnomethodology / Alain Coulon : translated from French by Jacqueline Coulon and Jack Katz.
        p.   cm. — (Qualitative research methods; v. 36)
    Includes bibliographical references.
    ISBN 0-8039-4776-3 (alk. paper). — ISBN 0-8039-4777-1 (pbk.: alk. paper)
    1. Ethnomethodology.   I. Title.   II. Series.
HM24.C677313   1995
306'.01—dc20   95-5586

            99   10   9   8   7   6   5   4   3

Sage Project Editor: Susan McElroy

CONTENTS

SERIES EDITORS' INTRODUCTION

Ethnomethodology is a mouth-filling word that is indexically peculiar when first encountered. In a personal way, it refers to the methods we have available to us to make sense of our immediate social surroundings and thus take action (and offer an account for such action) in league with our companions. As a research field, the term refers to the study of how members of an identified cultural or social group manage to make meaningful the varied worlds of their experience. The methods of interest to ethmetholologists are those commonplace and more or less taken-for-granted routines by which working definitions of social situations are collectively produced. Ethnomethodology is, then, the careful and systematic examination of the reality-generating mechanisms of everyday life—"the (study of) the ordinary methods that ordinary people use to realize their ordinary actions."

This concern for the ordinary must not mask or trivialize the extraordinary character of ethnomethodology. It is distinctive within the social sciences by purpose, language, sensitizing concepts, style, canonical writings, informing assumptions, philosophical grounding, studies topics, constitutive nature of its substantive findings, and so forth. Because of its paradigmatically distinct character, it has drawn critical fire; but ethnomethodologists respond by noting that social interaction and language use are most certainly the building blocks of any social order and for that reason alone deserve empirically detailed and systematic study.

Alain Coulon considers the aims and accomplishments of ethnomethodology in this, the 36th volume of the Sage series **Qualitative Research Methods**. In so doing, Coulon provides a crisp history of the growth of the field, an overview of the complementary, topical interest groups that now exist within the field, and a tidy assessment of some of the field's most impressive research findings. This work is, of course, a selective rendition of ethnomethodology, but it is one that fully appreciates—as will the reader on turning over the last page—the irony embedded in the great expectations of a field that must rest as a matter of principle on the locally produced, naturally organized, and reflexively accountable character of its own practical achievements.

—John Van Maanen
Peter K. Manning
Marc L. Miller

v

ETHNOMETHODOLOGY

ALAIN COULON
University of Paris VIII

Translated from French by
Jacqueline Coulon and Jack Katz

INTRODUCTION

Ethnomethodology is a current of American sociology born in the 1960s on the campuses of Californian universities. It spread to other American universities, then to European ones, especially English and German, and more recently French. Ethnomethodology was practically unknown to the French public until the publication, in the past few years, of some founding texts and comments, which have quickly multiplied.[1] But more than 25 years after Harold Garfinkel's (1967) founding work *Studies in Ethnomethodology*, the book still has not been translated into French. The few translations of ethnomethodological texts are scattered throughout some periodicals.[2]

The theoretical and epistemological importance of ethnomethodology is that it is a radical breach from traditional sociological modes of thinking. More than a constituted theory, it is a research perspective, a new intellectual posture. It constitutes a new paradigmatic map in the field of sociology and in the human sciences.

The arrival of ethnomethodology in sociological culture has brought a real upheaval in the sociological tradition, which takes place in a broadening of social thinking. Sociology that strives to comprehend is now being given more importance than sociology that strives to explain;

1

the qualitative approach to the social is being given more importance than the quantitative obsession of previous sociological research.

Ethnomethodological research is organized around the idea that we all are "practical sociologists," as Alfred Schütz says. The real is already described by the people. Ordinary language tells the social reality, describes it, and constitutes it at the same time.

Reacting to the Durkheimian definition of sociology, which is built on a breach from common sense, ethnomethodology shows that we have at our disposal the possibility of making an accurate account of what we do to organize our social existence. Analyzing ordinary practices in the always locally situated "here and now" of interaction, ethnomethodology joins other currents that have been kept outside official sociology, particularly the sociology of intervention, which also takes into account the fact that any social group is able to understand itself, to comment on itself, and to analyze itself.

The term *ethnomethodology* is not to be understood as a specific methodology of ethnology, nor as being a new methodological approach to sociology. Its origin is to be found, instead, in its theoretical conception of social phenomena. Let us try a definition: The scientific project of ethnomethodology is to analyze the methods, or the procedures, that people use for conducting the different affairs that they accomplish in their daily lives. Ethnomethodology is the analysis of the ordinary methods that ordinary people use to realize their ordinary actions. This lay "methodology"—what we are going to call ethnomethods—is used by the members of a society or of a social group in a banal but ingenious way to live together; these ethnomethods constitute the corpus of ethnomethodological research. Ethnomethodology can, then, be defined as the science of ethnomethods, that is, of the procedures that constitute what Garfinkel, the founder of the current and the creator of the word ethnomethodology, has called "practical sociological reasoning."

Ethnomethodology is not a marginal school. According to Richard Hilbert (1992), there is even a strong link between ethnomethodology and the classical sociology of Durkheim and Weber. In any case, ethnomethodology is not shaped out of the fields of research in social sciences. On the contrary, it has multiple links with research on such topics as interactionism, phenomenology, and existentialism, which nourish the contemporary milieu of reflection on our society.

1. THE FORERUNNERS

It is generally accepted that for Garfinkel, although not for other ethnomethodologists, the most important sources are the works of Talcott Parsons and Alfred Schütz. Parsons and Schütz were contemporaries, but their biographies were quite different. Parsons, born in the United States, developed an impressive body of work that soon influenced American social theory; Schütz, born in Austria, emigrated to the United States in 1939 when he was 40, and his influence remained limited until after his death in 1959. Except for a short period at the end of his life, Schütz was not a university teacher, but he presented papers at conferences, published numerous articles, and left a still-growing legacy in contemporary sociology.

Parsons and the Theory of Action

Parsons is one of the major figures in 20th-century American sociology. Opposing the mainstream sociology of his time, he rehabilitated European sociological theory by integrating works of Durkheim, Weber, Pareto, and others into a new "theory of action." Parsons was, at the time, a teacher in a great Department of Sociology at Harvard University in a period when students of sociology, social psychology, and anthropology were trained in a joint program. This training format enabled Parsons to be influential beyond the professional lines of sociology. Among the generation of American sociologists formed at Harvard during this period was Garfinkel.

In Parsons's theory, the actors' motivations are integrated in normative models that regulate behaviors and reciprocal appreciations. This integration is what accounts for the stability of social order and its reproduction in every individual encounter. As Parsons would see it, we share values that are beyond us and that rule us. To avoid anguish and sanctions, we tend to conform to the rules of common life.

How is it that we generally respect these rules of life in common, without even thinking about them? Parsons resorts to Freud to account for the regularity of social life: Freud showed that during education the rules of life in society are internalized by the individual and constitute what he calls *superego*, a sort of interior tribunal. According to Freud and Parsons, this internalized system governs our conduct and even our thoughts.

3

It is true that our communication is accomplished through systems such as language that on any occasion of use we draw on as preexisting, internal, endless, and stable resources. But ethnomethodology poses the problem differently: The relationship between actor and situation is not stable and unchanging, produced by cultural contents or rules; it is produced by processes of interpretation. This is a change of sociological paradigm: With ethnomethodology, we go from Parsons's normative paradigm to an interpretative paradigm.

Schütz

Schütz studied social sciences at the University of Vienna at the beginning of this century. Starting from reflections on the work of Max Weber, Schütz developed his first study (Schütz, 1932/1972). He sent this work to Husserl, who responded with the offer of a post as his assistant. Schütz declined the offer, but he kept a working relationship with Husserl until Schütz left Vienna permanently in 1938 to flee the Nazi regime. After spending a year in Paris, he settled in the United States, where he died in 1959. Only since his death has Schütz become regarded as a classic social thinker, but as early as the 1940s he gave lectures in New York, where Peter Berger and Thomas Luckmann were among his students.

Schütz's work of 1932, which founded sociological phenomenology, developed a new understanding of a classical sociological term. Although he had emphasized its importance, Weber had not clarified the notion of *Verstehen*, or understanding as opposed to explaining. Verstehen refers sometimes to commonsense knowledge and other times to a method specific to the social sciences. As his central idea and main contribution, Schütz developed the first meaning of Verstehen and proposed to study the processes of interpretation that we use in our daily life to give sense to our actions and to those of others. As Patrick Pharo (1985) emphasized, "it is the simple idea, found in Schütz, but also in a way in Wittgenstein," according to which "comprehension is always already accomplished in the most common activities of ordinary life" (p. 160). As Schütz noted, "everyday language conceals a treasury of pre-constituted types and characteristics, of social essence, that shelter unexplored contents." Schütz's social world is the world of daily life as lived by people who have no theoretical interest, a priori, in the constitution of the world. The social world is an intersubjective world, a world of routines, in which the acts of daily life are for the most part accomplished mechanically. Reality seems natural and obvious. For Schütz (1962), social reality is

> the sum total of objects and occurrences within the social cultural world as experienced by the common-sense thinking of men living their daily lives among their fellow-men, connected with them in manifold relations of interaction. It is the world of cultural objects and social institutions into which we are all born, within which we have to find our bearings, and with which we have to come to terms. From the outset, we, the actors on the social scene, experience the world we live in as a world both of nature and of culture, not as private but as an intersubjective one, that is, as a world common to all of us, either actually given or potentially accessible to everyone; and this involves intercommunication and language. (p. 53)

People do not, in any way, have identical experiences, but they suppose that their experiences are identical; they act as if they were, for all practical purposes, equivalent. The subjective experience of an individual is inaccessible to another individual. Ordinary actors themselves, although they are not philosophers, know that they never see the same objects in a common way: They do not have the same observational perspectives on these objects, nor do they have the same motivations, the same goals, or the same intentions when looking at them. At a football game, you do not see the same game if you are sitting in the center stands as if you are near the end zones. Everybody knows that and accepts that prices for tickets in these differing locations are not the same because of differences in the quality of the perspective. Yet everybody agrees that all spectators have attended the same match. In principle, that the actors do not see the same thing should prevent any possibility of a real intersubjective knowledge. Yet this is not the case, thanks to two "idealizations" used by the actors: that of the interchangeability of perspectives, on one hand (we can exchange seats and, doing so, exchange angles of view), and that of the conformity of the system of relevances, on the other (all spectators suppose that the others have come to see the game for the same reasons that they have, that they have the same interest in it or at least an identical empirical interest, in spite of biographical differences). Considered together, these two idealizations constitute "the general thesis of the reciprocity of perspectives," which marks the social character of the structure of *Lebenswelt* of each of us.

This description by Schütz enables us to understand how experiential, private, singular worlds can transcend into a common world: Because of these two idealizations, I can see the same thing that is seen by those sitting next to me at a game as well as by those who have not come to the stadium and are watching the game on television. We see the same match together, in spite of our different seats and our differences in sex, age, social status, and so on. In the same way, we both see the same bird flying, in spite of our differences of position in the space, our differences in sex and age, and in spite of the fact that you intend to shoot it when I only want to admire it.

By this permanent adjusting process, as expressed in these two idealizations, the actors succeed in dissipating their divergences of perception of the world. The "natural attitude" has an extraordinary capacity to construct the objects, and more generally, the actions and the events of social life, to maintain a common world. It also implies a capacity of interpretation such that the world is already described by the members in the very process in which it is perceived and experienced.

Symbolic Interactionism

Symbolic interactionism has been another source for ethnomethodology. The term was first used by Herbert Blumer in 1937. It had its origins in the "Chicago school of sociology" (Coulon, 1994), whose main representatives were Robert Park and Ernest Burgess (1921) and William I. Thomas (Thomas & Znaniecki, 1918-1920/1927). This current of thought popularized the use of participant observation as an accurate method of studying social reality, particularly the fast social changes that characterized the growth of Chicago. Symbolic interactionism takes a perspective opposite to that of the Durkheimian conception of the actor. Durkheim recognized the actor's capacity of describing the surrounding social facts, but he considered that those descriptions are too vague and too ambiguous to allow the researcher to use them scientifically. He claimed that these subjective descriptions do not belong to the field of sociology. Conversely, symbolic interactionism maintains that the conceptions that actors have of the social world constitute, in last analysis, the essential object of the sociological research (Blumer, 1969).

The methodological criticism made by the interactionists is radical. They reject the model of the quantitative survey and its claims of rigor and causal explanation in the social sciences. Accurate sociological knowledge cannot be developed through the use of methodological principles that would extract data from their context in order to make them objective. The use of questionnaires, interviews, attitude scales, calculations, statistics, and so on all create distance and move the researcher away, in the very name of objectivity, from the social world he or she wants to study. This scientific conception obviously produces a curious model of the actor, which has no relationship to the natural social reality in which the actor lives.

According to interactionists, authentic sociological knowledge is given to us in the immediate experience of our daily interactions. A researcher must first take into account the points of view of the actors under study, because it is through the meaning that they assign to objects, to people, and to the symbols that surround them that the actors build up their social world.

Some sociologists have at times disparaged the methodological and theoretical contributions of symbolic interactionism, contemptuously suggesting that it is a type of journalism with no genuine scientific status. Commonly, interactionism is assigned a role in the preliminary stages of investigation. Yet interactionism is deeply rooted in the traditions of American sociology and continues to exert influence, as can be seen especially in the study of deviance.

The importance of symbolic interactionism is considerable, not only because it insists on emphasizing the creative role played by actors in the construction of their daily lives but also for its particular attention to the details of this process. It should not be believed that interactionism is only a "wild sociology," without any theoretical hypotheses. It is founded on a very vivid theoretical tradition that seeks to understand how social objects are constructed. The social significance of objects (other people, material things, or collective phenomena like a group) comes from the fact that they are given sense in the course of our interaction. Even if some of these significances are stable over a period of time, they still have to be renegotiated at each new interaction. The world of social symbols is defined as a negotiated, temporary, fragile order, which has to be continually reconstructed to interpret the world. This constructivism, close to Marx's thought, is found in social phenomenology as well as in ethnomethodology, although in another form.

Labeling theory, which is a part of symbolic interactionism, takes to an extreme this orientation according to which the social world is not given but is constructed "here and now." Take, for example, the labeling of people as deviant. For the interactionist, deviance is not considered to be a "quality," an inherent characteristic of the person, or something that is produced by the deviant. On the contrary, deviance is understood to be created by a group of instituted definitions, by the reaction of authority to more or less marginal acts; in short, as the outcome of a social judgment. As Howard Becker (1963) put it:

> Deviance is *not* a quality of the act the person commits, but rather a consequence of the application by others of rules and sanctions to an "offender." The deviant is one to whom that label has successfully been applied; deviant behavior is behavior that people so label. (p. 9)

In other words, an individual does not become a deviant only through the accomplishment of an act. Deviance is not an inherent part of behavior.

The deviant is the one who has been caught, defined, isolated, designated, and stigmatized. It is one of the strongest ideas of labeling theory to think that social control, by labeling some persons as deviants, confirms them as being deviant because of the stigma attached to this labeling. This has sometimes been put so strongly as to suggest that social control paradoxically generates and reinforces deviant behaviors, when it has been originally instituted to combat, channel, and repress them. In an extreme version: People become what they are described to be.

For ethnomethodologists, who sometimes make use of labeling theory, deviance is not unilaterally defined as disobedience to norms. They consider it as the effect of a social construction, a production both by those who take care of the deviants and who label them, and by the deviants who label themselves as being deviant, confirming by their subsequent conduct the initial social labeling.

2. HISTORY OF THE
ETHNOMETHODOLOGICAL MOVEMENT

Ethnomethodology begins with the work of the sociologist Garfinkel. Born in 1917, he started university studies at Harvard in 1946, under the direction of Parsons. At the same time, he studied phenomenology, reading Husserl, Aron Gurwitsch, Maurice Merleau-Ponty, and Schütz.

1949: Interracial Crimes and the Definition of the Situation

Garfinkel published his first article, concerning inter- and intraracial homicides, their trials, and their judicial resolutions, in 1949. Garfinkel borrowed from Thomas the idea that actors take an active part in the "definition of the situation." To say that people, during their interactions, define the situation means that they are always defining, in their daily lives, the institutions in which they live. As Erving Goffman later emphasized, the "frame" of action has to be defined to act and to understand the actions of others. Unlike sociological analysis that seeks to explain how people act in situations prior to their encounters that are defined by others, ethnomethodology tries to understand how people see, describe, and jointly develop a definition of the situation (Zimmerman & Wieder, 1970).

1952: The Dissertation of Harold Garfinkel

In 1952, Garfinkel submitted his doctoral dissertation (Garfinkel, 1952). Parsons had a decisive influence on him that he never ceased to recognize. Although Garfinkel was not a "disciple" of Parsons in the sense of being a follower, he always admitted his debt:

> [My works] originated from my studies of the writings of Talcott Parsons, Alfred Schütz, Aron Gurwitsch and Edmund Husserl. For twenty years their writings have provided me with inexhaustible directives into the world of everyday activities. Parsons' work, particularly, remains awesome for the penetrating depth and unfailing precision of its practical sociological reasoning on the constituent tasks of the problem of social order and its solutions. (1967/1984, p. ix)

After completing his dissertation, Garfinkel took a teaching position in Ohio. In 1954, after conducting a study of trial juries, he went to the

University of California, Los Angeles, where he is still teaching. At UCLA, Garfinkel met Dell Hymes, who became one of the founders of the ethnology of communication. At the time, Garfinkel worked at the National Institute of Mental Health and began work at the UCLA Medical Center. Here he learned about the case of Agnes, a transsexual who became the object of one of his best known studies. Garfinkel influenced a number of students at UCLA.

In 1956, he published a study on degradation ceremonies (Garfinkel, 1956), which has an orientation reminiscent of a theme that Jean-Paul Sartre developed long before when he contrasted essentialist philosophy and existentialist philosophy. Garfinkel criticized the concept of "essences," which he said is not a scientific concept but a construction of daily life. This constructivism, which is related to pragmatism and to symbolic interactionism, became a central theme of the newly developed ethnomethodology. In 1959, Garfinkel participated in the Fourth World Congress of Sociology in Stresa, where he wrote a paper, subsequently published, whose title clearly displayed his intellectual preoccupations (Garfinkel, 1959).

Aaron Cicourel and the Constitution of the "Network"

In 1955, Aaron Cicourel, who would play a decisive role in the history of ethnomethodology, received a master's degree at UCLA. In 1963, he published, with John Kitsuse, a study on educational decision makers (Cicourel & Kitsuse, 1963). The following year, his work on method and measurement in sociology was published (Cicourel, 1964). In 1965, with Garfinkel, he led an informal seminar. The seminar brought together Harvey Sacks, Lawrence Wieder, Don H. Zimmerman, and several anthropologists, among them Michael Moerman, Bennetta Jules-Rosette, and Carlos Castaneda. In 1965-1966, Cicourel was at the University of California, Berkeley, where his students included Roy Turner and David Sudnow. There were then exchanges between Berkeley and Los Angeles, where Garfinkel was still teaching. Garfinkel and Cicourel were at the time the two leaders of the movement. In the same period, Sacks, a graduate student of Goffman's who would remain in the history of social sciences, after Goffman's death in 1975, as the founder and leader of conversation analysis, started to play an important part. He organized a working group in Berkeley that studied the publications of Garfinkel and Cicourel. This group brought together Moerman,

Emanuel Schegloff, Sudnow, and Turner. All traveled from one campus to another in California, and they formed what Nicholas Mullins (1974, pp. 192-193) described as a "network." However, the center of the network, according to Mullins, appears to have been at UCLA around Garfinkel, in spite of the organizing talents of Cicourel, whose center at the University of California, Santa Barbara, became more and more important. Zimmerman joined the UCLA center with Sudnow in 1965, accompanied by other graduate students, including Castaneda and Moerman, and submitted his doctoral dissertation the following year.

The Intellectual Diffusion

At the end of the 1960s, the apparently antisociological character of ethnomethodology became visible in the context of a crisis in sociology and contemporaneous student protest and counterculture movements. The breach was particularly evident in the structural-functionalism of Parsons and Robert Merton, who had dominated the preceding generation of sociologists. Yet ethnomethodology still developed within several university departments of sociology and more widely, within national and international organizations of sociology, through their periodicals and conventions, despite the fact that the leaders of ethnomethodology remained relatively remote in their Californian fiefdoms.

At this point in history, a larger public developed interest in the intellectual directions of ethnomethodology, in part because of a simultaneous rise of interest in phenomenological sociology. When Schütz died in 1959 he left a relatively scattered body of work. His works have been published in the *Collected Papers*, edited by Maurice Natanson, with the first volume appearing in 1962. Berger and Luckmann published their well-known work on the social construction of reality in 1966 (Berger & Luckmann, 1966). The publication of the *Collected Papers* continued in 1964 and in 1968.

At the same time, a cognitivist orientation, strongly marked by linguistic research, developed around Cicourel. Cicourel worked with, among others, John Gumperz, an ethnolinguist. Studies were conducted on the acquisition of language and on the interpretive competence of children. Sacks began work that would lead to the conversation-analytic side of ethnomethodology. According to Mullins, the Californian network consisted of 25 members in 1964. Garfinkel published several important articles, among them his article about trust (Garfinkel, 1963). Several of his works would be collected in his *Studies in Ethnomethodology*, which Garfinkel eventually published in 1967, reputedly under the pressure of university promotion and at the pressing behest of his entourage.

1967: The Founding Book

In the preface to *Studies*, Garfinkel (1967/1984) announced the reversal of perspective that his research had led him to:

> In contrast to certain versions of Durkheim that teach that the objective reality of social facts is sociology's fundamental principle, the lesson is taken instead, and used as a study policy, that the objective reality of social facts as an ongoing accomplishment of the concerted activities of daily life, with the ordinary, artful ways of that accomplishment being by members known, used, and taken for granted, is, for members doing sociology, a fundamental phenomenon. (p. vii)

Contrary to Durkheim, social facts do not impose themselves on us as an objective reality. The sociology postulate thus becomes with Garfinkel that social facts have to be considered as practical accomplishments; the social fact is not a stable object, but is produced by the continual activity of people, who make use of know-how, procedures, and behavior rules, in short, a lay methodology, the analysis of which constitutes the real task of the sociologist.

The following year, a critique and counteroffensive by conventional sociologists started with an article by James Coleman (1968).

Growth of the Movement

At the end of the 1960s, a new generation submitted doctoral dissertations on the Californian campuses, especially at Santa Barbara around Cicourel, who had established an impressive group of dissertation students. Pierce Flynn (1991) distinguishes four generations of ethnomethodologists, from 1950 to the 1980s. According to Flynn (p. 44), 16 doctorate degrees were completed between 1967 and 1972: Wieder in 1969; Hugh Mehan (1971), whose dissertation was on the educative interactions in a class; Marshall Shumsky (1972), who completed his doctorate on Californian encounter groups, based on his experience as an organizer in one of these groups; Robert McKay, who wrote his thesis in the same period as did Kenneth Leiter, Kenneth Jennings, Howard

Schwartz, David Roth, Warren Handel, Houston Wood, and many others. In 1972, there were about 50 ethnomethodologists.

These years of the expansion and blooming of the movement were also marked by important publications, too numerous to list here. Among the essential contributions after *Studies* were books by Sudnow (1967) on the social organization of dying, by Cicourel (1968) on juvenile delinquency, and by Peter McHugh (1968) on "defining the situation." In 1970, Zimmerman and Melvin Pollner (1970) published an important article on the everyday world as a phenomenon. This article was often referred to at the time as the most systematic presentation of differences between the ethnomethodological perspective and the ways of standard sociology. The authors showed that professional sociology has its roots in lay sociology, that it finds "resources" there, which it uses in a noncritical way and out of which it shapes the topics of its works. The authors elaborate on the notion of the occasioned corpus, which defines the instituting practices that characterize a local situation.

From the 1970s on, ethnomethodology parted into two groups: the conversation analysts, who search in our conversations for the contextual reconstructions that enable us to pursue conversations and to give them sense; and a group of sociologists for whom the admitted frontiers of their discipline remain restricted to the more traditional objects studied by sociology, such as education, justice, organizations, administrations, and science.

In spite of, or perhaps because of, those links with the usual sociological activity, ethnomethodology became the object of a new and spectacular attack in 1975 from Lewis Coser, then president of the American Sociological Association (Coser, 1975). He presented the ethnomethodological current as a sect whose development could threaten the future of the whole of American sociology. Zimmerman (1976) and Mehan and Wood (1976) replied to these attacks the following year.

Diffusion Abroad

At about the same time, ethnomethodology began to have a real impact outside of California. It settled on the East Coast as a new generation of researchers (Alan Blum, P. McHugh, R. McKay, G. Psathas, and J. Coulter) obtained teaching positions in the departments of sociology at universities in New York and Boston.

Ethnomethodology also spread to England, in London and Manchester, where an important group of ethnomethodologists is now concentrated, among them Rod Watson, John Lee, Douglas Benson, John Hughes, Wesley Sharrock, Bob Anderson, Paul Drew, E. Cuff, J. M. Atkinson, and Graham Button; and Germany, with the development of an interested group at the University of Bielefeld. Its progression was much slower in other countries, such as Italy; however, a translated textbook was published (Giglioli & Dal Lago, 1983).

In France, there was a lag of a decade before ethnomethodology began to find its place in sociological culture. The first references were made in 1973 (Herpin, 1973; Veron, 1973). In 1981, C. Bachmann, J. Lindenfeld, and J. Simonin published a work titled *Language and Social Communication*, which devotes a chapter to ethnomethodology. A few dissertations of ethnomethodological inspiration were submitted only after 10 more years (Ogien, 1984; Paperman, 1982; Pierrot, 1983). In the mid-1980s, some periodicals, although not the main sociological journals, devoted special issues to ethnomethodology. It began to be taught at the Maison des Sciences de l'Homme in Paris and in some universities, particularly Paris VII (ethnology) and Paris VIII (sociology, sciences of education—in which department I established a laboratory in 1988: Laboratoire de Recherches Ethnométhodologiques), and also Toulouse and Nice.

3. MAJOR CONCEPTS
OF ETHNOMETHODOLOGY

Garfinkel gave ethnomethodology a specific vocabulary. This vocabulary is not wholly new; ethnomethodology borrowed some of its terms from other fields: *indexicality* came from linguistics, *reflexivity* was taken from phenomenology, and the notion of "member" had been used by Parsons. Ethnomethodology has also given new meaning to terms taken from common language, like the notions of "practice" and "accountability." But what is immediately striking in ethnomethodology are the complementarity and the solidarity of its concepts. I have presented those that are most important and also most accessible.

Practice, Accomplishment

In the very first lines of the first chapter of *Studies*, "What Is Ethnomethodology?" Garfinkel (1967/1984) tells us that his studies

> seek to treat practical activities, practical circumstances, and practical sociological reasoning as topics of empirical study, and by paying to the most commonplace activities of daily life the attention usually accorded extraordinary events, seek to learn about them as phenomena in their right. (p. 1)

He declares his interests to be mainly in practical activities, particularly in practical reasoning, whether it be lay or professional.

Ethnomethodology is the empirical study of methods that individuals use to give sense to and at the same time to accomplish their daily actions: communicating, making decisions, and reasoning. For ethnomethodologists, sociology will therefore be the study of those daily activities, whether trivial or scientific, including sociology itself, which is appreciated as a practical activity. As George Psathas (1980) remarked, ethnomethodology is "a reflexive social practice seeking to explain the methods of all social practices, including its own." Unlike the sociologists who generally consider commonsense knowledge as "a residual category," ethnomethodology analyzes commonsense beliefs and behaviors as the necessary constituents of "any socially organized conduct."

Ethnomethodologists want to be closer to the common realities of social life than do other sociologists. They wish to attend more closely to experience, and this requires that they modify methods and techniques of data collection as well as elements of theoretical construction. Ethnomethodologists assume that everyday phenomena are warped when they are examined through "the grid of scientific description." Sociological descriptions typically ignore the actor's practical experience, and consider the actor himself to be an irrational being. Ethnomethodologists reject the traditional perspective of sociology on social reality. According to them, conventional sociologists make the a priori assumption that a stable system of norms and significations is shared by the actors and governs any social system.

The standard concepts of sociology, such as norms, rules, and structures, come from a theoretical framework that presupposes the existence of an outside signifying world that exists independent of social interactions. For sociology, these assumptions become in practice implicit resources.

What sociology names "models" is considered by ethnomethodology as a "continuous accomplishment of the actors." For ethnomethodology, even when the facts contradict their hypotheses, sociologists find ways of giving explanations that conform to their preestablished hypotheses, particularly that of the "stability of the object." According to Pollner (1974), ethnomethodology substitutes this hypothesis with that of process: "Where others might see 'things,' 'givens,' or 'facts of life,' the ethnomethodologist sees (or attempts to see) *process*: the process through which the perceivedly stable features of socially organized environments are continually created and sustained" (p. 27).

In a well-known article, Garfinkel and Sacks (1970) affirmed that "social facts are the accomplishments of the members" (p. 353). Social reality is constantly created by the actors; it is not a preexisting entity. This is why, for instance, ethnomethodology pays so much attention to the way the members make their decisions. Instead of making the assumption that the actors follow rules, the interest of ethnomethodology is to uncover the methods with which the actors "actualize" those rules. These methods are what make rules observable and capable of being described. The practical activities of members, engaged in their concrete activities, reveal the rules and the processes that can be studied. In other words, the careful observation and analysis of the processes used in the members' actions will uncover the processes by which the actors constantly interpret social reality and invent life in a permanent tinkering. Therefore, it is crucial to observe how, in a commonsense manner, actors produce and treat information in their exchanges and how they use language as a resource; in short, how they build up a "reasonable" world to be able to live in it.

Indexicality

Social life is constituted through language—not the language of grammarians or linguists but that of daily life. People speak, they get orders from others, they answer questions, they teach, they write sociology books, they go shopping, they buy or sell, they lie or cheat, they participate in meetings, they are interviewed—all with the same language competence. It is from this consideration that the ethnomethodological interrogation has developed.

In their descriptions and interpretations of social reality, sociologists use the same resources of language as do ordinary people, the common language. Sociologists spend their time "seeking to remedy the indexical properties of practical discourse" (Garfinkel & Sacks, 1970, p. 339). The idea that the expressions of ordinary language are indexical does not originate with ethnomethodology. Indexical expressions are expressions, such as "that," "I," "you," and so on, that draw their meanings from their context. They have long been the preoccupation of logicians and linguists. Indexicality is all the contextual determinations that are implicitly attached to a word. Indexicality is a technical word adapted from linguistics. It means that although a word has a transsituational signification, it also has a distinct significance in each particular situation in which it is used. The comprehension of a word requires "indicative characteristics" and demands that people "go beyond the information given to them" (Bar Hillel, 1954).

Indexicality points to the natural incompleteness of words, that words only take their complete sense in the context of their actual production, as they are "indexed" in a situation of linguistic exchange. And even then, indexing does not eliminate possible ambiguities in their potential meanings. The significance of a word or an expression comes from contextual factors such as the speaker's biography, his immediate intention, the unique relationship he has with his listener, and their past conversations. It is the same with the interviews or questionnaires that are used in sociology: The words and the sentences in them do not have the same meanings for all, and yet the "scientific" treatment by the sociologist of those interviews is done as if a semantic homogeneity of the words and a common agreement of the individuals over their meanings existed. Natural language, with all its situational contingencies, is a compulsory resource of any sociological survey.

For Garfinkel, the characteristics of indexical expressions have to be applied to the whole range of language. His conviction is that the entire corpus of natural language is deeply indexical, in the sense that for every member the significance of daily language depends on the context in which the language appears. Natural language cannot have meaning independent of the circumstances of its use and utterance.

Wilson and Zimmerman (1979-1980, pp. 57-58) gave the example of the enigmatic word *rosebud*, uttered by Kane on his deathbed in *Citizen Kane*, the film by Orson Welles. The film director takes the spectator along various paths of interpretation that turn into dead ends, and when the spectator, like the characters in the film, is about to give up trying to understand the significance of rosebud for Kane, the spectator is shown, in the very last seconds of the film, a glimpse of the word inscribed on Kane's childhood sled, which in the final scene is burning in a fireplace after having been discarded by movers who are cleaning out Kane's mansion. It is only then that the spectator catches the meaning and the poignant character of Kane's last word, that is, only after the spectator has erred in endless and unsatisfying interpretations because he was taken by the irretrievably indexical character of language and action.

Let us notice here that fiction masterpieces, whether on film or in novels, always play on the immense, irreducible indexicality of language and situations. The filmmakers and the novelists who are considered the best seem to be those who play the best with these indexical phenomena, that is, those who enable us, because they do not saturate their discourse, to use our imagination.

This notion of indexicality has been transposed by ethnomethodology to the social sciences. It means that all the symbolic forms, such as utterances, gestures, rules, and actions, have a "fringe of incompleteness," which disappears only when they are performed, although the completions themselves announce a "horizon of incompleteness" (Mehan & Wood, 1975, p. 90). Social situations that are the stuff of daily life have an endless indexicality, and the sociologist has "an infinite task of substitution of objective expressions to indexical expressions" (Pharo, 1984, p. 152).

A particular expression from common language, "et cetera," has been minutely analyzed by several ethnomethodologists (Bittner, 1963; Cicourel, 1970; Sacks, 1963). It is often a complement to a demonstrative expression, meaning: "you know what I mean, I do not have to insist, to name with precision all that has to do with what I have just been saying, you can easily complete it for yourself, carry on with my demonstration, find other examples to my enumeration, et cetera." The rule of "et cetera" implies that a speaker and a listener tacitly accept and assume together the meaning of what is said by treating their descriptions as obvious, even if they are not immediately obvious. It means that a common, socially distributed knowledge exists. This is what Cicourel (1972) called "the retrospective-prospective character of events":

> Vague or ambiguous or truncated expressions are located by members, given meaning contextually and across contexts, by their *retrospective-prospective sense of occurrence*. Present utterances or descriptive accounts that contain ambiguous or promissory overtones can be examined prospectively by the speaker-hearer for their possible meaning in some future sense under the assumption of filling in meanings now and imagining the kinds of intentions that can be expected later. Alternatively, past remarks can now be seen as clarifying present utterances. The filling in and connecting principles enable the actor to maintain a sense of social structure over clock and experienced time despite deliberate or presumed vagueness and minimal information conveyed by participants during exchanges. (p. 87)

For the logicians, indexical expressions are considered inconveniences because they forbid one to use general propositions to decide whether something is true, because to do that one must ignore the contextual circumstances of their production. Hence the frequent attempts of the sociologists, and especially of the anthroposocial sciences, to take out indexical expressions to replace them with objective expressions. But this is a difficult, even impossible, task, because how may one decide that an expression is indexical and that another is objective? This is why Garfinkel, even though he did not introduce the concept of indexicality, suggested that we consider it in a different way. Indexical expressions are not parasitic expressions in the course of our daily conversations. On the contrary, they constitute the discourse itself, which is built up through their usage. Everyday language has an ordinary meaning that people have no difficulty in understanding. The intelligibility of our exchanges, instead of suffering from their indexical nature, depends on it, and it is the knowledge of the circumstances for properly executing an utterance that enables us to give our expressions a precise meaning. So, instead of criticizing ordinary language for its failures when evaluated on formalistic methodological principles, Garfinkel proposed to study language use, regarding its indexical character not as a flaw but as one of its main characteristics, and seeking to know how we use ordinary language by employing, in a routine and trivial way, indexical expressions.

Indexicality also means that the sense of talk is always local and that generalization about the meaning of a word is impossible, contrary to what the anthroposocial sciences would like us to believe. This means that a word, because of the circumstances of its utterance, and an institution, because of the conditions of its existence, can be analyzed only in reference to the situations of its use. Therefore, the analysis of these indexical situations is endless: "The attempt to 'clean' the world of indexical expressions, which is an attempt to substitute 'objective' expressions for indexical ones, becomes a topic for description and analysis rather than an effort to solve a problem" (Benson & Hughes, 1983, p. 115).

Reflexivity

Wieder (1974b) presented the following case:

Pablo is detained in a center of rehabilitation for drug addicts. He dreads retaliation from another drug addict, who is due to arrive at the center. Pablo is panicked, in fear that the newcomer might think he is an informer. Several years before, they took and sold drugs together; they were both arrested, but only his companion was condemned. Therefore, Pablo believes that the other must think he has denounced him, even though this is not true. He wants to leave the institution to avoid retaliation, including retaliation from the current inmates, who, if they learn about his so-called informing, will beat him and maybe even kill him.

Pablo's "confession" took Wieder (1974b) on the track of the implicit code used by the inmates. Wieder indeed discovered, at the beginning of his study of the institution, the existence of such a code. This code exists in all detention centers, but he had never had the opportunity, except with the Pablo case, to analyze informer cases to see how the code worked. But Pablo, in an interview, tells an educator: "You know I won't snitch."

The inmates talked easily of this code, which was a real moral order that regulated their daily conducts. They also talked of the sanctions applied to "kiss asses, snitches, and snivelers." This code, constantly enforced but never put into such words by the inmates, mainly concerned informing but also covered refusing to complain about the thefts of which they were victims, sharing or selling drugs to the other inmates, helping others satisfy their deviant behaviors, never trusting the educators, and so on. The rules of the code become conduct rules: For instance, not to inform meant keeping at a distance and defying the wardens to show the others that there was no chance of informing one day, as might have been implied had one adopted a cordial attitude toward the wardens. This is a nonverbal way of telling the code.

Wieder (1974b) illustrated what he calls a *reflexive formulation* (p. 152), taking up this expression from Pablo: "You know I won't snitch." The analysis of this utterance shows several elements:

1. It told what had just happened, for example, "you just asked me to snitch."
2. It formulated what the resident was doing in saying that phrase, for example, "I am saying that this is my answer to your question. My answer is not to answer."
3. It formulated the resident's motives for saying what he was saying and doing what he was doing, for example, "I'm not answering in order to avoid snitching."
4. It formulated the immediate relationship between the listener and teller by relocating the conversation in the context of the persisting role relationships between the parties, for example, "For *you* to ask *me* that, would be asking me to snitch."
5. It was *one more* formulation of the features of the persisting role relationship between hearer and teller, for example, "You are an agent and I am a resident-parolee. Some things you might ask me involve informing on my fellow residents. Residents do not inform on each other. We call that snitching."

We can say that the first elements refer to the interaction and the second to the institutional context establishing the relationships between roles, according to Parsons (1937). But as Widmer (1986) noted, if those aspects pointed out by Wieder's analysis remind us of a conventional sociological analysis, Wieder's perspective is still distinctively ethnomethodological. What has been revealed by the analysis remains largely implicit in the answers of the youths. What has been revealed is not a substantive code but a way of actualizing the code, and the practice of the code is only made necessary because of the researcher's efforts to understand it and by the interaction between the researcher and the inmate. Just as the codification of the sorcery knowledge of Don Juan as described by Castaneda (1972a) is an analytical translation of a vernacular knowledge, so the analysis of the law of silence is a scientific, analytic discourse on a sort of secret language of the forbidden, which translates the implacable law of the group of delinquents. This is a law that is actually only formulated in a concrete interaction.

Wieder (1974b) first presented the law of silence of the youths of the center as a sociologist would, in describing the informal laws as parts of "deviant subcultures." But then he stressed the reflexive interactional aspect of these formulations. The code does not exist outside of the situation in which one tries to uncover it. The interaction with the researcher in which the researcher is not told about the code itself "tells" the code. The code is not the object of conversations, of fashionable comments between the inmates. The code is generally tacit, but at the same time it structures the situation. It can only emerge in what is not said in language. The code of secrecy is an injunction to hide that only pertains when there is an effort to discover.

Reflexivity must not be mistaken with reflection. When it is said that people have reflexive practices, it does not mean that they think about what they are doing. Members have no awareness of the reflexive character of their actions. They would be incapable of pursuing engaged practical action if they were to maintain an awareness of the reflexive character of their action. As Garfinkel (1967/1984) emphasized, members are not interested in practical circumstances and in practical actions as topics of direct discussion. They do not seek to theorize:

> Not only do members take that reflexivity for granted, but they recognize, demonstrate, and make observable for each other the rational character of their actual, and that means their occasional, practices while respecting that reflexivity as an unalterable and unavoidable condition of their inquiries. (Garfinkel, 1967/1984, p. 8)

Instead of regarding reflexivity as an obstacle to maintaining and comprehending social order, Garfinkel, on the contrary, made it a primary condition.

Reflexivity, therefore, refers to the practices that at once describe and constitute a social framework. Reflexivity is that feature of social action that presupposes the conditions of its production and at the same time makes the act observable as an action of a recognizable sort. In the course of our ordinary activities, we do not pay attention to the fact that while we are talking, we are building up—at the same time that our words are uttered—the meaning, the order, and the rationality of what we are doing. The descriptions of the social world become, as soon as they have been uttered, constitutive parts of what they have described.

To describe a situation is to constitute it. Reflexivity refers to the equivalence between describing and producing an action, between its comprehension and the expression of this comprehension. "Doing" an interaction is telling it. Reflexivity presupposes "that the activities whereby members produce and manage settings of organized everyday affairs are identical with members' procedures for making those settings 'account-able' " (Garfinkel, 1967/1984, p. 1).

Accountability

In his preface to *Studies*, Garfinkel (1967/1984) wrote: "Ethnomethodological studies analyze everyday activities as members' methods for making those same activities visibly-rational-and-reportable-for-all-practical-purposes, i.e., 'accountable,' as organizations of common place everyday activities" (p. vii). Louis Quéré (1984) emphasized "two important characteristics of accountability: it is reflexive and it is rational. To say that it is reflexive is to emphasize the fact that the accountability of an activity and of its circumstances is a constitutive element of those activities" (p. 104). To say that it is rational, "is to emphasize the fact that it is methodically produced in situation, and that the activities are intelligible, that they can be described, and evaluated under the aspect of their rationality" (Quéré, 1984, p. 105).

Quéré borrowed from Garfinkel four examples of accountability: the study of the Suicide Prevention Center (SPC) in Los Angeles, the case of Agnes, the discovery of the optical pulsar, and an ordinary conversation reported and analyzed in *Studies*. I examine the first two examples in this chapter; I deal with the two others when the fields of application of ethnomethodology are presented.

The study of the activities of the SPC appears in Chapter 1 of *Studies*. This center makes inquiries, when requested by a judge, about cases of unnatural death. It must establish whether the death is due to suicide or to some other cause. Garfinkel wanted to know if the inquiries by the staff of the SPC are comparable, in their commonsense and lay sociology processes, to the deliberations of the jury of Wichita, to the selection of the patients for a psychiatric treatment, or to the processes of coding the content of medical files by sociology students as well as to "the innumerable professional processes used in an anthropological, linguistic, psychiatric, or sociological inquiry." In the conclusion to this chapter, Garfinkel indicated some recommendations that constitute an important methodological element in ethnomethodological research.

Quéré (1984) commented on those recommendations by emphasizing that there are two levels of analysis: that of the self-organization of the SPC and that of the accounts, that is, of the representation of the other.

> At a first level, the S.P.C. organizes itself practically as an ordered, objective reality, with a finality, with rationality and coherence. . . . This self-organization is expressed by material arrangements, by a division of labor, by the definition of inquiry processes, of processes of constitution and revision of files, of processes of archiving, by the accumulation of resources (information network, address books, etc.). At a second level, the organization builds up, through practices of investigation and interpretation of itself, accounts in which it is represented as objective reality, in which it is given an identity, a finality and a structure of order (rationality, coherence, efficiency . . .). (Quéré, 1984, p. 104)

One has to understand that ethnomethodologists seek to define and theorize accountability, to tell in what way the accounts are "informing" or "structuring" of the situation of utterance (Zimmerman & Pollner, 1970).

The second example proposed by Quéré is the story of Agnes, the object of Chapter 5 of *Studies*.

Agnes is a 19-year-old transsexual secretary who had chosen to become a woman and asked to be operated on at the UCLA Medical Center in 1958. In this case, Garfinkel intervened as an expert in the context of a research project on transsexuality that was organized by the hospital. He had 35 hours of interview time with Agnes. Garfinkel showed that Agnes must continuously exhibit, in all the activities of her daily life, the cultural characteristics of a "normal" woman. This production of her woman-being is a continuous practical accomplishment, never completed, because she has not mastered a routine femininity. On the contrary, she must continuously control her attitudes, when she eats, when she goes to the beach, when she has to hide from her roommate. In these respects, she shows, as Simone de Beauvoir has put it, that "you are not born a woman, you become one." Generally, we are born with a male or female body, but then we have to become a boy or a girl culturally, and at the same time exhibit the accomplished character of masculinity or femininity.

Here, "accountability" is this "exhibition" of a sexual personality in daily activities and conduct. It is a renewed declaration, which is generally lived as natural and handled as a routinized matter. But Agnes has to check her presentation of self to appear as the "real thing." She is abnormally self-conscious about the process. The work of constituting the sexuality in each of us is usually hidden, and forgotten; as with Marx, the producers forget the production of the merchandise in the process of reification (Gabel, 1975). This reification and forgetting happen because "society hides from its members its activities of organization and thus leads them to see its features as determinate and independent objects" (Garfinkel, 1967/1984, p. 182).

To say that the social world is accountable means that it is describable, intelligible, reportable, and analyzable. All of these features are revealed in the practical actions of the people. The world is not given once and for all, it is constituted in our practical accomplishments. As Zimmerman (1976) put it, ethnomethodologists

> treat members' accounts of the social world as situated accomplishments, not as informants' inside view of what is "really happening." Ethnomethodology's concern, in general, is the elucidation of how accounts or descriptions of an event, a relationship, or a thing are produced in interaction in such a way that they achieve some situated methodological status, e.g., as factual or fanciful, objective or subjective, etc. (p. 10)

Contrary to what is sometimes asserted, ethnomethodologists do not regard actors' accounts as descriptions of social reality. The analysis of these accounts is only useful for them insofar as it reveals in what way actors permanently reconstruct a fragile and precarious social order to understand each other and to be able to communicate. The property of these descriptions is not to describe the world, but to permanently reveal its constitution. It is this meaning that has to be given, in all ethnomethodological studies, to the expression "account": If I describe a scene of my daily life, it is not because it describes the world that an ethnomethodologist can be interested in but because this description, by accomplishing itself, "makes up" the world or builds it up. Making the world visible is making my action comprehensible in doing it, because I reveal its significance through the exposition of the methods by which I make an account of it.

The Notion of Member

In the ethnomethodological vocabulary, the notion of *member* does not refer to a social category but to the mastery of natural language:

> The notion of member is the heart of the matter. We do not use the term to refer to a person. It refers instead to mastery of natural language, which we understand in the following way.
>
> We offer the observation that persons, because of the fact that they are heard to be speaking a natural language, *somehow* are heard to be engaged in the objective production and objective display of commonsense knowledge of everyday activities as observable and reportable phenomena. (Garfinkel & Sacks, 1970, p. 339)

It seems that Garfinkel has gone from the Parsonian conception of the notion of member, which insisted on "collectivity membership" (1967/ 1984, footnotes pp. 57, 76), that is, belonging to a community, to a more linguistic conception, which emphasizes the mastery of the natural language.

More recently, in an interview with Jules-Rosette (1985), Garfinkel explained again the concept of member and went further than he did in 1970 from the Parsonian definition of the member:

> I am talking of local production and of naturally available and accountable social order. Our inquiries bring us back unavoidably to Merleau-Ponty to relearn what he has taught us: our familiarity with society is an ongoing miracle without cease or time out. That familiarity, as we conceive it, covers the ensemble of daily life accomplishments as practices which are

fundamental to any form of collaboration and interaction. We have to talk about practices which, as vulgar competence, are necessary for the constitutive production of the everyday phenomena of social order. We refer to these competences by introducing the notion of "members."

Using the notion of member is not without risk. In its most common use, it is worse than useless. It is the same with the concepts of "particular persons" or "individuals." Some sociologists insist that we have to conceive of members as individuals collectively organized. We firmly reject this allegation. For us, "persons," "particular persons," and "individuals" are observable features of ordinary activities.

To become a member is to become affiliated to a group, to an institution, which requests the progressive mastery of the common institutional language. This affiliation lies on the uniqueness of each individual, on his or her unique way of managing the world, of "being-in-the-world," in the social institutions of daily life. Once they are affiliated, the members do not have to think about what they are doing. They know the implicit conditions of their conduct, and they accept the routines woven into the fabric of everyday social practices. This is why one is not a stranger to one's own culture, and why, conversely, the behaviors or the questions of a foreigner may seem strange.

A member is not only a person who breathes and who thinks but a person with a whole ensemble of processes, methods, activities, and know-how that enables her to invent adjusting devices to give sense to the surrounding world. It is a person who, having embodied the ethnomethods of a particular group, "naturally" exhibits the social competence that affiliates her with this group, allowing her to be recognized and accepted.

4. LAY SOCIOLOGY AND PROFESSIONAL SOCIOLOGY

In 1967, a 2-day symposium at Purdue University brought together 20 sociologists who had come to discuss ethnomethodology (Hill & Crittenden, 1968). During this conference, Garfinkel was invited by the chairman to specify the relationship between ethnomethodology and traditional forms of ethnographic study and to explain the origin of the word.

Garfinkel explained that in 1954 he began working on a study of court jurors with Fred Strodtbeck and Saul Mendlovitz, who were then teaching at the Law School of the University of Chicago. Strodtbeck had secretly put microphones in the deliberation room of a court in Wichita, Kansas, to record the jurors' deliberations. Garfinkel was struck by the fact that the jurors, although they had no judicial training, were able to consider an offense and to judge the innocence or guilt of the accused. To do so, they used commonsense processes and logic: By making a distinction between the true and the false, and between the probable and the likely, they were able to assess the accuracy of the testimony given during the trial:

> They were concerned with such things as adequate accounts, adequate description, and adequate evidence. They wanted not to be "commonsensical" when they used notions of "common sensicality." They wanted to be legal. They would talk of being legal. At the same time they wanted to be fair. If you pressed them to provide you with what they understood to be legal, then they would immediately become deferential and say "Oh, well, I'm not a lawyer. I can't be really expected to know what's legal and tell you what's legal. You're a lawyer after all." (p. 6)

In a way, those were assessment and judgment practices, which were describable, but for which Garfinkel had no proper term yet. He "found" the term ethnomethodology some time later, in 1955, it seems, and he told how chance helped him to find it, not through his work about the jurors' deliberations, but in reading ethnographic documents:

> I was working with the Yale cross-cultural area files. . . . I came to a section: ethnobotany, ethnophysiology, ethnophysics. Here I am faced with

jurors who are doing methodology, but they are doing their methodology in the "now you see it, now you don't" fashion.

Now, how to stick a label on that stuff, for the time being, to help me to recall the burden of it? How to get a reminder of it? That is the way "ethnomethodology" was used to begin with. "Ethno" seemed to refer, somehow or other, to the availability to a member of common-sense knowledge of his society as common-sense knowledge of the "whatever." If it were "ethnobotany," then it had to do somehow or other with his knowledge of and his grasp of what were for members adequate methods for dealing with botanical matters. Someone from another society, like an anthropologist in this case, would recognize the matters as botanical matters. The member would employ ethnobotany as adequate grounds of inference and action in the conduct of his own affairs in the company of others like him. It was that plain, and the notion of "ethnomethodology" or the term "ethnomethodology" was taken in this sense. (pp. 7-8)

Thus the jurors used ethnomethods, that is, a commonsense logic that they possessed and "embodied" and that is not the judicial logic of a specialist, borrowed for the circumstances.

This led Garfinkel to distinguish two complementary meanings of the word ethnomethodology. First, he directly links his new term to other, established, terms that are well known in anthropology, such as ethnomedicine, ethnobotany, and so on. Just as botany is the area of members' understandings that ethnobotany studies, so methodology, in the term ethnomethodology, is the member's understanding that Garfinkel wished to frame for investigation. These members' methodologies, which Garfinkel frequently referred to as "practical sociological reasoning," become the focus or target of ethnomethodological research. Thus ethnomethodology took a focus on the methods that people use to enable them to recognize each other as living in the same world. Second, the jurors, Garfinkel found, had valid methods that were available to them as members of the daily moral life of their society. These methods are local, specific to a "tribe," and they are not immediately accessible to a stranger to that tribe. By calling them ethnomethods, Garfinkel sought to indicate that members belong to specific groups, to local organizations or institutions. Ethnomethodology then became the study of the methods that member use in their daily lives that enable them to live together and to govern their social relationships, whether conflictual or harmonious.

Practical Knowledge
and Scientific Knowledge

The production of the visibility of social order entails a process of objectification that is not the monopoly of scientific activity. For ethnomethodology, scientific activity is itself the product of practical knowledge, which itself can become an object of research for sociology. Garfinkel's sociology "is instituted on the admittance of the reflexive and interpretative capacity of any social actor" (Ogien, 1984, p. 62). The practical knowledge mode is

> the ability to interpret that any individual, scientific or lay, is possessed of and uses in the routines of his daily practical activities. . . . This process is ruled by common sense, the interpretation is indissociable from the action and equally shared by the ensemble of the social actors. . . . The scientific knowledge mode is not to be distinguished from the practical knowledge mode, when one considers that they are confronted to a similar problem to be solved: none of them can occur without the mastery of a "natural language" and without using a whole series of indexical properties that are part of it. (Ogien, 1984, p. 70)

In fact, for the ethnomethodologist, the epistemological gap between practical and scientific knowledge is not of the same nature as the one generally admitted by sociologists.

The Social Actor Is
Not a Judgmental Dope

Garfinkel reversed the relationship of the actor to his milieu; he undermined the tendency of sociology to oppose the hidden to the manifest. For sociology, the meaning of members' actions is only accessible to the professional sociologist. He alone, like the psychoanalyst with his patient, would be able to elucidate the social secret of human conduct. The actor would ignore the source of his daily actions, he would not know that he goes to the museum or that he makes photos because he belongs to the middle class. Thus the sociologist treats him, as Garfinkel put it, as "a judgmental dope": "The sociologists conceive the man-in-society as a judgmental dope . . . who produces the stability of society by acting in conformity with preestablished and legitimate action alternatives, which culture provides him with."

Objectivism and Subjectivism

We can illustrate the ethnomethodological reversal by using terms that are not Garfinkel's, but that can indicate the polemical place of ethnomethodology in sociology:

Objectivism isolates the object of research; it introduces a separation between observers and observed by relegating the searcher to an outside position. This epistemological break is judged necessary for the "objectivity" of the observation; the researcher's subjectivity is denied or said to have been halted during the time of research. Subjectivity is considered, in deference to objectivity, to be a parasite of the process of research. The objectivist tradition chooses objects of research that accept the constraints of the methods of observation, which are conducted typically to produced quantified data; they reflect an obsession with precise measurement. There is in this style of work a global conception of the frame of analysis, a conception that is based on the idea that a preestablished order is reproduced by the researcher, an order in which the actors being studied are not conscious of the significance of their acts. The objectivist treats the "fixity," the universality, and the relative stability of this order as what makes it analyzable.

Subjectivism takes the opposite course: The object is not an isolated entity but is always interrelated with the person who studies it. There is no epistemological break; the necessary objectification of practice takes into account the researcher's many interests. The researcher's subjectivity is appreciated and analyzed as a phenomenon that belongs naturally to the field under study. It is heuristic to consider the researcher's subjectivity. The methods used by subjectivists are usually forms of qualitative analysis, in which the unique can be significant, as can phenomena that are nonmeasurable. The framework of social action results from a continuous construction, from a permanent creation of the norms by the actors themselves. Subjectivism rehabilitates the transitory and the singular.

Fundamentally, objectivism and subjectivism disagree about the nature of social action and about the role attributed to the actor. Is he manipulated without his knowledge by determinisms on which he has no grasp? If so, the sociologist's work would consist of revealing the hidden significations, or driving out the clandestine work of social determinism. Or is the actor, as ethnomethodology has it, capable, in the course of his daily activities, of reasoning, understanding, and interpreting his actions? If so, the sociologist would have to analyze the perspective of the actor in the course of his daily activities. In short, does the actor act, or is he acted on?

The consequences of this tension in the field of sociology can be easily guessed. Objectivism and subjectivism have two opposite views of institutions: One defines the institution as a social form defined independent of the actors, as an ensemble of norms that are imposed on them; the other reverses the relationship that the members have with their institutions and sees them as building up institutions in a process of permanent tinkering. These questions are fundamental. The epistemological opposition that they imply is not new. It has long been at the origin of sociological reflexion: two conceptions of science, of practice, of rationality, of the relationship of the actor to this rationality, and to the significance of his or her actions.

For ethnomethodologists, there is no difference in nature between, on one hand, the methods used by the members of a society to understand each other and to understand their social world and, on the other, the methods used by the professional sociologist to attain a knowledge, which claims to be scientific, of the same world. Garfinkel (1967/1984) demonstrated this continuity between lay and professional sociology by an experiment presented in a chapter of *Studies*.

The Documentary Method of Interpretation

Garfinkel borrowed from Mannheim the notion of "documentary method of interpretation," a notion that, in his *Essays on the Theory of Knowledge*, Mannheim had reserved for scientific knowledge. Garfinkel (1967/1984) showed that this documentary method is already in action in lay sociology; that is, it is operative in the processes through which people understand each other and are able to investigate their daily world:

> The method consists of treating an actual appearance as "the document of," as "pointing to," as "standing on behalf of" a presupposed underlying pattern. Not only is the underlying pattern derived from its individual documentary evidences, but the individual documentary evidences, in their turn, are interpreted on the basis of "what is known" about the underlying pattern. Each is used to elaborate the other. (p. 78)

Thomas Wilson (1970) summed up the documentary method as follows:

> Documentary interpretation consists of identifying an underlying pattern behind a series of appearances such that each appearance is seen as referring to, an expression of, or a "document of," the underlying pattern. However, the underlying pattern itself is identified through its individual concrete appearances, so that the appearances reflecting the pattern and the pattern itself mutually determine one another in the same way that the "part" and the "whole" mutually determine each other in Gestalt phenomena. (p. 68)

"Pattern" has to be understood as something that is accountable, that is, reportable-observable-describable, something that refers to a meaning and therefore to a process of interpretation. As Jacqueline Signorini (1985) emphasized:

> The pattern is the topic but it is also the process of enunciation—to say, and how to say: the biographical elements which two persons have in common, the unease, the complicity, the conduct of family life . . . the pattern belongs to the elements of common sense knowledge, to the socially sanctioned facts. The accountability of a pattern is presumably known by all. That is why, in the organization of a practical activity such as conversation, a pattern is constantly referred to, to understand the elements of details, the indexicals of the conversation. From this point of view, the language is the natural place of exhibition and production of the patterns. (p. 78)

Indeed, we are always seeking patterns in the conduct of our daily conversations, otherwise, our exchanges would be meaningless. The underlying patterns have to be imperatively summoned to compensate for and to try to remedy the indexicality of language. Furthermore, this is true not only of language. The documentary method of interpretation enables us to see the actions of others as the expressions of patterns, and these patterns enable us to see what these actions are. Individuals unveil social reality to each other, making it "readable" by building up visible patterns. The actions are continuously interpreted in terms of context, the context being in its turn understood through those actions. This is what enables us to retrospectively reinterpret some scenes and to modify our judgment about things and events.

Garfinkel said that this "method" makes it possible to know what another person is talking about, because this person never exactly says what he or she means. It is also used by professional sociologists:

The documentary method is used whenever the investigator constructs a life history or a "natural history." The task of historicizing the person's biography consists of using the documentary method to select and order past occurrences so as to furnish the present state of affairs its relevant past and prospects.

The use of the documentary method is not confined to cases of "soft" procedures and "partial descriptions." It occurs as well in cases of rigorous procedures where descriptions are intended to exhaust a definite field of possible observables. (Garfinkel, 1967/1984, p. 95)

An Experiment

The functioning of the documentary method of interpretation was clarified in a laboratory experiment. Garfinkel (1967/1984) invited 10 students to take part in an experiment that consisted of studying "alternative means to psychotherapy 'as a way of giving persons advice about their personal problems' " (p. 79). Each student was counseled individually by an experimenter, who was falsely presented as a student counselor. After having presented the context of the problem about which he wished to be advised, the student had to ask the "counselor" at least 10 questions, to which the experimenter could answer yes or no. Once the first question had been asked, the experimenter, who was in the next room, answered yes or no through an intercommunication system. The student had then to unplug the system of communication so that the counselor "would not hear his remarks." (The comments made by the student about the exchange were taped.) Once he had finished his remarks, the student plugged the system in again and asked his next question. This process continued until the end of the interview. The student then had to summarize his impressions of the entire exchange; finally, he was interviewed.

The counselor's yes or no answers were in fact predecided according to a table of random numbers. However, the students always considered them, even when they were surprising and contradictory, answers to the questions.

For instance, a Jewish student asked in an "interview" to be advised on the behavior he has to adopt because his girlfriend is not a Jew and he dare not expose the situation to his father (Garfinkel, 1967/1984, pp. 80-85). Although they were randomized, the subject understood the experimenter's answers as answers to his own questions. He caught what "the adviser had in mind" and understood "at a glance" what the experimenter was talking about, that is, what he meant.

What concerns the student at the beginning of the interview is that his girlfriend is not, like him, Jewish. And the elements of the context, which he is going to document thanks to the advice, are the intentions and the attitudes of his parents, particularly his father. These elements are the field of his interpretation. His interpretation of his father's disapproval documents the disapproval, as a perceived fact to which the student gives reality, in making his problem describable. "It is noticeable that, from the start, the student supposes that the experimenter has at hand the elements of common sense knowledge that subjects referred to as 'shedding new light' on the past" (Garfinkel, 1967/1984, pp. 89-90).

From the first question, which is related to the problem of continuing his relationship with the girl, to which the experimenter answers no, one can see how the interpretation functions. Instead of understanding the "no" as related to the question he asked, as related to his girlfriend, he interprets it as related to his father's supposed disapproval. The "no" becomes a "yes," which documents the fear of the father's feeling. Suppositions are used to make the interpretation possible. The interpreted fact gets in the future a reality that it has not acquired in the present.

As the student's comments after the interview clearly indicate, this case shows that the effort by the student to analyze, interpret, and document the various aspects of his problems is based on the implicit use of a commonsense knowledge that, he supposes, is shared by the experimenter. This also shows, as psychoanalysis already understands, that the advice is built up by the subject, not by the adviser or the psychoanalyst. It is a question of interpreting commonsense data, specifically, of gathering, classifying, and eliminating and sometimes "rearranging" the elements of the context. The subject consults the supposed significations of the adviser's answers and endlessly gives sense to randomized answers. It is the subject who produces and operationalizes the advice, not the adviser.

All the students who had taken part in the experiment felt that they had really been advised. The subject had no difficulty in continuing the exchanges, in going to the end of the planned series of questions that were obviously not preprogrammed. When the answers appeared unsatisfying to them, subjects waited for later answers in order to decide the sense they could attribute to the previous.

> Over the course of the exchange, subjects sometimes started with the reply as an answer and altered the previous sense of their question to accommodate this to the reply as the answer to the retrospectively revised question. . . . The same utterance was used to answer several different questions separated in time. Subjects referred to this as "shedding new light" on the past. . . . Incongruous answers were resolved by imputing knowledge and intent to the adviser. (Garfinkel, 1967/1984, pp. 89-90, 91)

This commonsense knowledge, which the subject and the adviser are supposed to share, Garfinkel called a "scheme of interpretation." It is constituted by facts socially sanctioned. By implicitly referring to these organized facts of the social system, the actors prove their belonging in a cultural and social community that allows them to document certain problems and gives them the meaning resources that make the interpretation of these problems possible. The common knowledge has to be understood as a structured ensemble of facts.

Talking about the documentary method of interpretation thus means that the actors use the current events as resources to interpret past actions and to discover and give them new significations. Several characteristics are significant in this process. On one hand, the student creates meaning from his interpretation of the experimenter's yes or no, which he feels provides genuine advice. On the other hand, he constantly chooses elements from the context to pursue his interpretative process. Last, he constantly builds up the reference frame of the pattern.

Signorini (1985) showed how this phenomenon functions when she talked of her work when programming computers: "Programming is to produce the structure of the thought. Thus there is no difference between saying 'I' and 'I have an idea.' The thought and the object of the thought are the same thing. We cannot attain the thought, the 'I,' but only structured products" (p. 102).

We often use this method in our daily exchanges. It is not only encountered in experimental situations such as the case that was studied by Garfinkel (1967/1984, pp. 38-39), who showed that the method functions all the time in our daily life, as in the ordinary conversations that husband and wife have. It is this method that enables us to reconstitute the meaning of a conversation whose beginning we have missed, that gives sense to gestures, and so on. We are doing this work of documentation every time we have to decide the meaning of a word in a context. We select, modify, and give order to potential meanings as the conversation, which is fed by our infinite interpretations, goes on. It is endless work: In other experiments, the students were unable, whatever the elaboration and the sophistication of their comments, to give a univocal and significant description of what was understood in a part of the conversation they had had.

Professional Practice

These reflexions can be generalized and applied to sociological reasoning and practice. Garfinkel (1967/1984) thought that "examples of the use of the documentary method can be cited from every area of sociological investigation":

> Its use is found also on the many occasions of survey research when the researcher, in reviewing his interview notes or editing the answers to a questionnaire, has to decide "what the respondent had in mind." When a researcher is addressed to the "motivated character" of an action, or a theory, or a person's compliance to a legitimate order and the like, he will use what he has actually observed to "document" an "underlying pattern." The documentary method is used to epitomize the object. (pp. 94-95)

For instance, in the interviews, the interviewer uses "a set of *ad hoc* tactics for adjusting to present opportunity" (p. 98).

Much of core sociology consists of "reasonable findings." Many, if not most, situations of sociological inquiry are commonsense situations of choice. We constantly employ these elements in the course of our inquiries to understand what has been said. A real event is at once interpreted to document the circumstances of the present situation. Documentary work establishes a correspondence of meaning between a real and a supposed occurrence, so that the latter appears as evident, as the verification of what is studied. Thus it is not the fact, as is presented to us, that is analyzed, but past occurrences of the same fact or of similar ones—reasonable, commonsense "documents" of these facts. This explains why, as Garfinkel remarked, we sometimes decide to wait for the future developments of a situation to check that those futures are informed by the present situation. Then we start a piece of retrospective inquiry work, making imputations about the future to make sense of the present. This work evokes the work done by Agnes: Having changed sex, she uses her present appearance as a resource to interpret the past and to discover new significations that might be used in her new apprenticeship in "being-woman."

The work of the documentary method of interpretation is this never-ending work of putting into perspective, of evaluating the potentialities, and of taking into account circumstantial conditions, which the actor undertakes to understand his action as well as that of others.

Practical Sociological Reasoning and Conversation Analysis

One of the most developed and richest fields of ethnomethodology is undoubtedly conversation analysis (Boden & Zimmerman, 1991; Drew & Heritage, 1992; Psathas, 1995; Sacks, 1992; Schegloff, 1968, 1990). It has even sometimes been considered to be an autonomous field, separate from ethnomethodology, because it is far from the usual sociological inquiry. But conversation analysis can be considered the most accomplished program of ethnomethodology and constitutes a current of its own in sociology. This practice, founded by Sacks in the mid-1960s, is evidently central, as it concerns—because the very objects of its research are verbal exchanges and ordinary conversations—all of the other fields that ethnomethodology has been interested in. It also concerns other fields of social and human sciences. Although language is constantly at the core of the problem of data collection, sociology has not taken it as a topic for study. Sacks, Schegloff, and their followers, on the other hand, used conversation as the central topic of their research.

Conversation analysis is the study of the structures and the formal properties of language considered in its social use. To be able to go on, our conversations are organized; they respect an order, which is not necessary to explain in the course of our exchanges, but which is essential to make them intelligible. In other words, we show, in the course of our conversations, our social competence in exchanging with others, by making comprehensible to others our behaviors and by interpreting theirs. The utterances are locally organized, giving us the thread of the conversation and enabling us to understand it and pursue the exchange. We are constantly using these processes in our conversations. They are not the only ones: For instance, we talk in turns and questions and answers are paired, which Sacks called "adjacency pairs." We use other participants in the conversation when we invite somebody, or when we greet someone, or when we want to cut short a lengthy conversation.

With John Heritage (1984, chap. 8), we can summarize the three main hypotheses of conversation analysis as follows:

1. Interaction is structurally organized.
2. The contributions of the participants to this interaction are contextually oriented: The indexing process of utterances to a context is inevitable.
3. These two properties are actualized in every detail of the interaction, so that no detail can be disposed of as being accidental or inaccurate.

Sacks has shown the importance of the context in the following example of interaction:

A: I have a 14-year-old son.
B: All right.
A: I also have a dog.
B: Oh! I am sorry!

This exchange can be understood only if we know that A is a prospective renter negotiating with B, the owner of the apartment. The theme of the conversation is constructed by the partners. The context makes the exchanges coherent and intelligible.

The agreement over the construction of the meaning, however, is not always that simple. It can be the occasion of numerous negotiations. Zimmerman (1987) demonstrated this point by analyzing the misunderstandings and the ensuing quarrel that arose during an emergency telephone call. The analysis of the conversation, automatically recorded by an emergency service, enables us to understand how the situation of misunderstanding and quarrel is constructed. The discussion is a struggle for influence. Its analysis reveals the bureaucratic routines of the emergency service, but also the caller's background expectancies. Furthermore, on hearing the tape, the protagonists' voice intonations may suggest that the nurse is black and the man calling is a homosexual. These elements may have been used by the participants to the exchange to document their understandings of what was going on.

This shows that the forms of the exchange determine its comprehension, which is intersubjectively constructed. In the field of language as well as in others, we find in conversation analysis the constant preoccupation of ethnomethodology with describing the processes that we use to construct the social order. Bernard Conein (1987) demonstrated this point in quite a different field, through an analysis of the conversations exchanged in a strike committee during the student unrest of December 1986 in France:

> A grammar of action can emphasize the competence of the participants in producing political actions. . . . The political competence is part of the common knowledge of the social structure. This competence has to be described, and not constructed. (pp. 59, 63)

5. QUESTIONS OF METHOD

There is a common misunderstanding of the term ethnomethodology. It is sometimes believed that the claim is of a new methodology of ethnology. This is not so. We have seen that the term has to be understood, according to Garfinkel, as the science (logos) of ethnomethods, that is, of the procedures that constitute what he called "practical sociological reasoning." How is one to start the study of ethnomethods, if that is the object of ethnomethodology? Is there a new "methodology"?

The "Ethnomethodological Indifference" Posture

Ethnomethodologists do not believe that the behaviors and the activities of an individual are directly governed by his or her social position. They think that sociologists have "over socialized" the behavior of actors. They reject the hypothesis of the internalization of norms—that norms provoke conduct automatically and nonreflectively—on the grounds that such a view does not give an accurate account of the way the actors perceive and interpret the world, recognize the familiar, and construct the acceptable. Nor does the traditional view explain how rules concretely govern interactions. Garfinkel (1952) noted the matter in his dissertation: "The empirical world of the sociologist is inhabited by types" (p. 222). The actor, as observed by the sociologist, is fake; he is a construction whose rationality has no other goal than to verify the pertinence of the model. The sociologist's actor has no biography, no history, no passions. Above all, he is incapable of judgment. Garfinkel's criticism is radical. As we have seen, for him, professional sociologists and commonsense actors construct their worlds in the same way.

[Analysis] is not the monopoly of philosophers and professional sociologists. Members of the society are concerned as a matter of course and necessarily with these matters both as features and for the socially managed production of their everyday affairs. The study of common sense knowledge and common sense activities consists of treating as problematic phenomena the actual methods whereby members of a society, doing sociology, lay or professional, make the social structures of everyday activities observable. (Garfinkel, 1967/1984, p. 75)

Professional sociology is a practical activity like any other and can be analyzed as a practice. For that reason, it has sometimes been said that ethnomethodology is simply a sociology of sociology. The project of ethnomethodology is more subtle. By insisting on the commonsense foundations of professional sociology, by considering it as a "folk discipline," ethnomethodology becomes an intimate part of the reality it proposes to study. Sociological research relies on a tacit, commonsense vision of the world. Even statistics, which have often been regarded and used as reliable indicators, directly depend on the judgment capacities of the actors who collect the data.[3] Sociology supposes that social reality exists independently from the research of which it is the object. This is the reason why sociological investigations often develop "reasonable findings" and produce "documentary work" (Garfinkel, 1967/1984, pp. 99-100). For the ethnomethodologists, sociology has hardly gone beyond the stage of the "natural attitude" of phenomenology. Its practice has remained naive. As Garfinkel noted in the preface to *Studies*:

> There can be nothing to quarrel with or to correct about practical sociological reasoning. . . . Ethnomethodological studies are not directed to formulating or arguing correctives. They are useless when they are done as ironies. Although they are directed to the preparation of manuals on sociological methods, these are in *no way* supplements to "standard" procedure, but are distinct from them. (p. viii)

Garfinkel and Sacks (1970) defined what has to be understood by "ethnomethodological indifference":

> Ethnomethodological studies of formal structures are directed to the study of such phenomena, seeking to describe members' accounts of formal structures wherever and by whomever they are done, while abstaining from all judgments of their adequacy, value, importance, necessity, practicality, success, or consequentiality. We refer to this procedural policy as "ethnomethodological indifference." (pp. 345-346)

Experimental Breaching

In *Studies*, there are many observations and even experiments, such as the famous breaching experiments, which consist of upsetting our routines. These routines are founded, as Parsons noted, on a moral order that is necessary to the accomplishment of our actions. This necessity of a moral order, which guarantees the success of the interactions, has its ethnomethodological transposition in the Garfinkelian notion of "trust," which is the title of an article by Garfinkel (1963). In this article, he made use of the analysis of experimental breachings in games to show, through the breaching, the moral background of common activities. If with Parsons, the parties to games conform to external social rules that have been internalized by education, according to Garfinkel the background models are what enable us to interpret the actions of the partners. For instance, Garfinkel showed that if you and I are playing cards, we naturally have first accepted in common the rules of the game. If I leave the room, the rules are simply suspended until I return, and we are still in a relation of trust. But if I breach the rules in a provocative way—and this I can do to experiment with the background of trust—I provoke a scandal that reveals the necessity of an a priori trust, without which the social relationship could not be durably maintained. The scandal is not so much in the breaching of the rules of the game as in the breaching of the trust, which is the fundamental condition, usually hidden, of the game with its accepted rules.

The totality of these procedures does not constitute a new set of field techniques. The techniques used by Garfinkel, and later by his disciples, are the methods of modern qualitative sociology. Therefore, searching for precepts to study the social facts would be in vain. Garfinkel has warned us about it: It is not a matter of correcting the procedures of standard sociology, nor of writing a new chapter of methodology for the existing sociology books. However, the critique of traditional sociology methods, particularly of quantitative methods, is an important part of the foundations of ethnomethodology. The first and the most famous critique of those methods is Cicourel's (1964) book about method and measurement in social sciences.

Methodological Contribution of Cicourel

Cicourel was the first important disciple of Garfinkel. Soon he became his collaborator and the coleader of the ethnomethodological school. In 1964, he published an important work that provided an epistemological base for the field, as its ambition is to show the interactions between theory, methods, and data (Cicourel, 1964). Cicourel proposed to restart sociological research by critically examining the foundations of method and measurement, constantly keeping in mind, as MacIver (1942) put it, that "the social structure is mainly created" (pp. 20-21).

Cicourel argued that the methodological decisions made in social sciences research have theoretical counterparts, and that the theoretical assumptions underlying methods and measurement in sociology cannot be separated from the language used by sociologists in their theorizing and research reports. The first task of the sociologist is, therefore, to clarify the language that he or she uses. Sociological research requires a theory of instrumentation and a theory of data, so that one may distinguish the observer's procedures and intervention from the material that he or she calls data.

A question is also raised in Cicourel's (1964) book about the common use of mathematical and measurement systems in social sciences research. Cicourel insisted that he does not mean that sociocultural facts cannot be measured by existing mathematical methods, but that the fundamental facts of social action should be clarified before irrelevant measurement postulates are imposed.

The first chapter examines in detail the problem of measurement. Its principal argument is that current measurement devices are not relevant because they impose numerical procedures that are external to the social, observable world as described by the sociologist, as well as to the concepts founded on those descriptions. If this reflection was carried to its extreme, it might suggest that because the concepts on which sociological theories are founded have not, in essence, any numerical properties, it would be impossible to know which numerical properties are to be sought in reality. Cicourel does not adopt such an extreme position in his following chapters, which are, in succession, about participant observation, interviews, multiple-choice questionnaires, demographic method, content analysis, experimental research, and linguistics. He does not suggest that sociologists should stop any research and measurement until they have clarified the fundamental categories of daily life. His point is not to try to improve the systems of measurement to make them "better" but to consolidate the methodological foundations of sociological research. According to Cicourel, sociologists do not give enough importance to the study of "subjective" variables, particularly those that contribute to the contingent character of daily life.

Ethnomethodology, Constitutive Ethnography, and Qualitative Sociology

In practice, when conducting field research ethnomethodologists are obliged to borrow research devices from ethnography, because they have not produced an original technology. To illustrate the point, I present two contributions: that of Mehan about constitutive ethnography, more specifically applied to education but generalizable to other fields, and that of Zimmerman, which he calls "tracking."

CONSTITUTIVE ETHNOGRAPHY

Mehan (1978) proposed a new approach, inspired by ethnomethodology, which he calls "constitutive ethnography." According to him, "constitutive studies operate on the interactional premise that social structures are social accomplishments" (p. 36). We have here one of the founding principles of ethnomethodology, whereby "the social facts are practical accomplishments."

> The central tenet of constitutive studies of school is that "objective social facts," such as students' intelligence, scholastic achievement, or career patterns, and "routine patterns of behavior," such as classroom organization, are accomplished in the interaction between teachers and students, testers and students, principals and teachers. Rather than merely describe recurrent patterns of behavior or seek correlations among variables, constitutive analysts study the structuring activities that construct the social facts of education. (Mehan, 1978, p. 36)

Beyond this theoretical orientation, four main principles characterize constitutive ethnography:

— The ability repeatedly to consult the data (audio or video documents for instance, or integral transcriptions);

— The thoroughness of the treatment of the data, which is a means of counteracting the tendency to exploit only the elements that are favorable to the researchers' hypotheses;

— The convergence between researchers and participants about their perspectives of the events, with the researchers making sure that the structure that they reveal in the members' actions is the same as the one that orients the participants in those actions; in this regard, "elicitation devices" are used to verify with the people studied that the frames of analysis are correct;

— The interactional analysis, which avoids psychological reduction, as well as sociological reification.

Because the organization of events is socially constructed, the structuring of action will be sought in the participants' expressions and gestures.

In the field, ethnomethodologists adopt the methods employed by other qualitative or clinical sociologies. The data collection devices used by ethnomethodologists are extremely varied: direct observations in classes, participant observation,[4] interviews, examination of administrative files and school reports, study of testing results, video recordings of classes or counselings, sessions showing video recordings to the actors themselves, and recordings of comments made during these showings. These methods are related to ethnography, whose primary methodological precept is field work, the observation of the actors in situ.

Beyond these techniques of data collection, the researchers who conduct constitutive ethnography adopt a specific posture of research, which is summed up by Mehan (1971, p. 22) in his dissertation: Because the institutional conditions of research have a major influence on the research itself, they constitute one of the research materials. This principle is not as banal as it first seems, because it recognizes the indexical or contextual character of any social fact.

This has also been noted by another researcher, Steve Woolgar, who, in the ethnomethodologically inspired study he made with Bruno Latour on life in a research laboratory (Latour & Woolgar, 1979), has created what he called "reflexive ethnography." The purpose of reflexive ethnography is to take into account simultaneously the object of research and the way the research is done, with the hypothesis that they are both not only linked but that knowledge of one enables the researcher to understand the other better.

The integration of the research diary into the research report itself, by taking into account negotiations with members that led to the analysis of the setting, is at the heart of various forms of reflexive socioanalytical theory. We find the same idea in Castaneda's (1972b) dissertation, which is constituted by the diary of the researcher's search for the secret of hallucinogen plants.

Another characteristic of Mehan's research work, as reflected in his dissertation, is the abandonment of the traditional "hypotheses-before-going-in-the-field." The research team, led by Cicourel (Cicourel et al., 1974),[5] did not very well know what to search for at the start. They wanted to study lessons in classes, but as Mehan (1971) wrote:

> We could only use vague descriptive terms like "we want to look at the way you teach the children, the kind of style you use"; "we want to see how you decide whether a child's answer is correct or incorrect"; "we want to see if your vocabulary matches the vocabulary of the children in the class." Vague descriptions were necessary because we really *couldn't* tell the teacher what we wanted until after we saw it, and, also, because we were afraid of contaminating her presentation. If she knew exactly what we wanted, we were afraid she would begin producing instances of that phenomenon, either to please us, or as an unintended consequence of that knowledge. (pp. 25-26)

An essential feature of ethnomethodological practice is to seek to discover rather than presume the description of the matters it would study. Because ethnomethodology aims at showing the means used by the members to organize their social life in common, the first task of an ethnomethodological research strategy is to describe what the members do. Consequently, this implies the deliberate choice of localism, which is fully consistent with a scientific practice of sociology.

TRACKING

Zimmerman (n.d.) introduced a notion of tracking that differed from its general usage in the American educational system, where the term has generally meant classifying pupils along ability and curriculum lines. Zimmerman takes the term in the colloquial sense of the hunter, as in following someone's tracks.

For Zimmerman, because the researcher is an individual within the collectivity, the researcher must take into account his own involvement in his research strategy. On the other hand, acquiring "an intimate view of a particular social world" implies sharing a common language with the members to avoid misinterpretations. Catching the members' point of view does not simply consist of listening to what they say or asking them to explain what they do. It implies locating their descriptions in their generative context and considering the members' accounts as research instructions.

The practice of showing an interest in the members' point of view is often regarded as the sign of a subjective approach. Zimmerman reminds us that the notion of member has to be interpreted in the ethnomethodological sense: A member is one who possesses a "mastery of the natural language," a taken-for-granted social competence to participate in the collectivity in which the individual lives. One has to keep in mind the principle of the ethnographic interview, which consists of obtaining from an informer the socially sanctioned knowledge of his community: His descriptions and his explanations are regarded as valid and accurate by the other competent members of the community. The information collected has to be "intersubjectively validated." This does not mean, in any way, Zimmerman insisted, that there is a transfer of competence from "the analytical authority toward the subjects of the research."

Penetrating into the community that one proposes to study requires that one have a strategy of introduction, the details of which must vary with the field and the research. But one has to give particular attention, Zimmerman (n.d.) said, to the framing of what I would call the observation and research device: "The ethnographer has to find the means of being where he needs to be, of seeing and hearing whatever he can, of developing trust between him and the subjects, and of asking numerous questions."

Naturally, the ethnographer has to succeed in getting from the collected information the meaning of the observed events. To do so, an obvious resource is what the people say. People are commenting on their activities all the time. For instance, in a university the students are always talking about their courses, their teachers, their university work, but also about their weekends. To grasp the meaning of their talk, it is necessary to describe the repetitive occurrences and the routine activities of group members. To do so, it is necessary to be both in an external position and to be a participant in the natural conversations in which the significations of the routines of the participants emerge.

Tracking is one of the features of participant observation. It consists in observing as many situations as possible in the fieldwork. Through tracking, the researcher tries to see what the subject sees. The research takes on the style of reporting. When, for instance, the research is about police activities, these activities can be described as routine activities if one shadows the policemen, as Raymond Depardon did in *Faits divers* ("News item"). This film, with its telling title, can be regarded as an excellent illustration of ethnomethodological questioning. Ethnographic tracking is an answer to the problem of the position of the observer in front of the diversity of the social behaviors. Not only does it enable him or her to observe social behaviors but also to find out what the participants say about them. Naturally, this implies that the researcher can move freely inside his setting for research.

This strategy of research is based on the idea that the construction of the social world by members is methodical and may be discovered. This social world is based on common cultural resources, which enable members not only to construct it but also to recognize it.

The ethnomethodological doctrine is, as Mehan (1982) said, "fundamentally constructivist." The secret of social construction does not lie in the statistics produced by "expert" members and used by other "social experts" who have forgotten the statistics' reified character. On the contrary, it is revealed by the analysis of ethnomethods, that is, of the procedures that the members of a social form use to produce and to recognize their world and to make it familiar as they assemble it.

6. FIELDWORK

From the beginning of the movement, ethnomethodologists have devoted most of their studies to social problems. As we have seen, in his earlier writings Garfinkel was interested in the problem of trials and criminal justice. His work continued with studies about jurors' decision making and with research about suicide. All the dissertations that have been submitted in the ethnomethodological current deal, as has been seen, with a social problem along the lines generally borrowed from ethnography. But the break with positivist sociology is not located in field techniques: The break is in the fact that for each field studied, the ethnomethodologists emphasize the interactional activities that constitute the social facts.

Social facts are not objects but, in Garfinkel's language, practical accomplishments; this is the new sociological paradigm that is the outcome of a whole current in American sociology and that serves as a thread in every ethnomethodological field study.

The following fields are among the great domains of sociological investigation:

— Education, which has been the subject of many studies (Coulon, 1993); interactions in classes, the organization of lessons, testing and exam practices, counseling processes, the creation of inequality (Rosenbaum, 1976), and in higher education the apprenticeship of "learning" the job of being a student (Coulon, 1990);

— The judicial system, the courts and the prisons, as well as police practices, which are a particularly well-explored field of ethnomethodology: Bittner (1967), Garfinkel (1967/1984, pp. 104-115), Cicourel (1968), Emerson (1969), Sacks (1972), Wieder (1974a, 1974b), and Pollner (1974) described the practices used by the police to establish the "criminal facts" and by the judges and the courts as well as by attorneys to constitute the "judicial facts";

— Medical practices, particularly the organization of death in hospitals (Sudnow, 1967), the formal and informal categorizations of the patients (Garfinkel, 1967/1984, pp. 186-207), the diagnosis and medical practices, and aftercare and social work practices in psychiatric hospitals (Ogien, 1989);

— Organizational processes: Bittner (1965/1974) critically analyzed the concept of organization and the Weberian ideal-type, whereas Zimmerman (1969/1974) studied interactions within an organizational system;

— Scientific research: Garfinkel, Lynch, and Livingston (1981) studied the activities of the scientific research laboratory. Livingston (1978) wrote his thesis on the work of mathematicians, and Lynch (1979) studied the problem of the artifact in a scientific laboratory.

In addition, ethnologists such as Moerman (1968), Bellmann (1975, 1984), Jules-Rosette (1975), and Castaneda (1968) showed interest in ethnomethodological orientation, and Bittner (1963) studied radical political movements.

I now illustrate the range of ethnomethodological investigations by reviewing some of the fields that have been studied.

Education

Most studies in the sociology of education, wrote Mehan (1978), treat social structures as if they were constrained and objective "social facts." It is as though education, as a process, had been treated as a closed system, the analysis of which has been deliberately ignored, by investigators who have been interested only in the inputs and outputs of the system. At the entrance of the system, the researcher notes a certain number of factors (sex, age, parents' socioeconomic status, ethnicity); then he or she describes the patterns at the exit point, for example, school failures and dropouts, and concludes that "the son will do his father's job" and that inequality is reproduced. But such work does not demonstrate how this inequality is reproduced inside the closed system, that is, the school. Although educational interactions must play a major role in the outcomes they attempt to explain, sociologists of education have not examined the educational processes directly.

Mehan (1978) contended that the study of the concrete conditions in which the everyday education process occurs is necessary for anyone who wants to understand the influence of school on people's future lives. He wanted to demonstrate concretely how such factors as the number of pupils per class, the pedagogical methods, or the size of the classrooms "operate in practical educational situations." In the same way, the influence of such factors as social class, race, and teacher's attitude has to be shown in the situation itself, in the interactions between the partners within the educational act:

Students' performance in school is not independent of the assessment procedures that produce accounts of students' successes, abilities, and progress.

The constitutive analysis of the structuring of school structure has been conducted in school settings that typically have consequences for students' careers: classrooms, educational-testing encounters, and counseling sessions. In each case researchers have demonstrated that the educational facts peculiar to the settings are assembled in the interaction among the participants. . . . Constitutive studies of counseling sessions have examined how students' career choices are structured in the interaction between counselors and students during guidance interviews. (Mehan, 1978, p. 40)

INTERACTIONS IN THE CLASSROOM

When we observe a class, Mehan said, it appears to be organized: Teachers and students speak in turn, at precise moments. The students write, they work in small groups, or they read in silence. In short, we see a real social organization. It is of course an instituted order. What has to be analyzed is the way these institutions are born and structured. Mehan and his collaborators videotaped a class, with students of different ages and ethnicities, for a whole school year. They analyzed nine classes, and they showed that it is the interactional work between teachers and students that produces the class organization. Teachers and students mark the borders of interactional sequences, of thematic exchanges, of the phases and of the lessons themselves, by modifications in their gestures and by paralinguistic as well as verbal behaviors. The functions of these changes of behavior are to indicate to the partners where they situate themselves during their exchanges. They structure the exchange situation. We can say that they are markers of the situation. They enable each one to know where he stands in the temporality of the class.

By centering on the interactions that occur during the class, Mehan (1979, 1980) showed that a great number of activities simultaneously take place. The students consciously develop their own strategies to achieve goals independent from the teacher's and to carry on their own affairs. Thus the students show their "interactional competence." A certain number of rules are set by the teacher, such as "not to run in the class," "be clean," and "respect others," but none of these rules indicates when and how it has to be applied. The students have to find out in situ, in their interactions with each other and with the teacher, the signification and the functioning of these rules. A competent student is, therefore, one who can make a synthesis between academic content and interactional forms, which are necessary to the accomplishment of a task. Any separation between form and content is immediately interpreted by the teacher as the sign of incompetence. This should enable us to give a new definition to a student's ability, as ethnomethodological studies of exams and counseling have shown.

TESTING AND EXAMINATION

Mehan (1979, 1980) studied the way answers are produced during testing. I have shown already that the significance of questions is not the same for everybody, contrary to one of the founding hypotheses of the principle of testing. Their meaning is not shared by the testing adults and the tested children. What are considered wrong answers very often represent a different interpretation of the conceptual material and not a lack of knowledge nor an inability to reason correctly. Treating the testing results as objective facts hides the processes used by the students to construct their answers. Yet it is this very construction that should be judged as fundamental by educators, because its analysis would enable them to evaluate the real reasoning capacities of the students.

Mehan videotaped WISC (Weschler Intelligence Scale for Children) testing of rural children in Indiana. Formally, the testers are supposed to assign grades immediately after the student answers by assigning the answer a 0, 1, or 2, according to its quality; then the testers are supposed to proceed to the next question. The analysis of the video record showed that, in fact, the responses to 21 of 65 questions had been influenced by the tester's interventions. In these 21 cases, testers either repeated the question, gave indications as to the proper answer, or urged the student to give a second answer. Such intervention resulted in an elevation of the child's score from 1 to 2 in 50% of the cases. The final score of one student was 27% superior to what it would have been if the tester had not helped him. In another testing experience, the children, responding to the urgings of the testers, increased their correct answers by 44%.

Taking the testing results as an objective fact hides three mechanisms:

— The way the students interpret the questions and the material presented, to get the answer;
— The way a tester interprets and chooses what, among a variety of behaviors, constitutes an acceptable answer;
— The way testers and students jointly produce the answers during testing.

COUNSELING

Counselors play an important role in student guidance, particularly in high school. Cicourel and Kitsuse (1963) showed how arbitrary decisions, based on racism and socioeconomic prejudices, could be made by counselors in high schools with regard to admissions in colleges. Ethnomethodological works in education seek to analyze how these decisions, which are very important for the students' future, are made.

Frederick Erickson (1975) examined the role played by counselors in the process of advising students on courses and course sequences of varying ranks. After having worked as a counselor in a black suburb of a large American city, the practices involved in racial discrimination and differential selection, which he witnessed daily for 3 years, led him to question the role of counselors of all kinds. He came to see their role as maintaining the social order of the whites. Later, when he was a professor, he decided to analyze the encounters of the high school students with the counselors. The role of these counselors is ambiguous: They are at the same time the students' defenders and judges employed by the administration:

> To some students, school and society can be described as an open structure in which they will be able to decide what they want and act effectively to reach their goals. To others, the social structure can be presented as a closed one in which individuals do not choose for themselves, in which many hurdles and problems lie ahead. Depending on what counselors select to emphasize about society, students may experience counselors' advice as encouragement or as restraint. (Erickson, 1975, p. 46)

The counselors do not treat all students in the same way. Their interviews with students are supposed to be based on objective and universal criteria, but in fact, the participants, in the course of their interactions, constantly give particularistic information. Erickson noted that the students who established good rapport—by talking about themselves, their sport activities, and interests they have in common with their counselor—got more positive counseling. By minutely analyzing recordings of the interviews, he found that there was at times an embodied harmony—breathing with the same rhythm, harmonious and soft voices, synchronized gestures—between the counselor and the student.

The orientation decisions that are made during the interaction depend on the subjective judgment of the counselor and on his or her representation of the student. Some characteristics of the student are taken into account, others are not. They are arbitrarily, subjectively sorted out. The counselor will sometimes take into account a student's school marks, the way the student dresses, his athletic build; sometimes his race, sex, beauty, language; sometimes his ease, probable social class, distinction, and so on. Most of these attributes are determined by birth and have nothing to do with school merit. But the real process of selection disappears behind the counselor's diagnosis.

Thus ethnomethodological studies of the classroom and of the school as in institution help us understand the daily, ordinary mechanisms by which social stratification is created within the school itself. These mechanisms of "making inequality" are enacted in numerous interactional situations at school everyday. The stratification of students within the school, which feeds the reproduction of inequalities beyond the school, is not produced out of thin air. The ethnomethodological demonstration does not aim at accusing the educators, the counselors, or the school administrators, or at making them feel guilty; however, by giving them access to the mechanisms of the interactions, it could help modify them. The works of the sociology of education rarely escape an objectivist physicalism, which tends to represent the world as being constituted by a series of objective classifications, independent of the sociologist's intervention. That is why ethnomethodology seems so rich. By opening the closed system of the school, ethnomethodology reveals, as Mehan said, a whole interactional machinery, usually hidden, that is made up of verbal and nonverbal relationships. It shows how the "objective" educational facts emerge from structuring activities that are hidden in a process of reification. It shows "the steps whereby the society hides from its members its activities of organization and thus leads them to see its features as determinate and independent objects" (Garfinkel, 1967/1984, p. 182).

BEING A STUDENT IS A JOB

This phenomenon is particularly visible when one examines the affiliation practices that enable a freshman to learn his/her "job" when he/she changes from the status of high school pupil to the status of university student (Coulon, 1990). The affiliation is a process that consists of discovering and using the routines, the matter of course actions—the ethnomethods—that are hidden in the everyday practices in higher education. If he/she fails to do so, the freshman will be unable to join the new group, and will rapidly fail or drop out. I have shown that being unable to see, to decipher, and then to embody the hidden codes that regulate social relations in the university constitutes one of the main reasons for dropping out and for failing, phenomena that occur massively during the first year of university study in France. To succeed at a university, the freshman has to show competence as a student by learning to make practical use of the rules on which university work is based; the student must learn to use university rules metaphorically. A student reveals competence by showing that he/she has become a member. This is done by displaying that he/she can categorize the world in the same way as does the university community.

Juvenile Delinquency

Among the various ethnomethodological studies on delinquency, I have taken a detailed look at the study that Cicourel (1968) made in two Californian towns for 4 years. In this study, he aimed at demonstrating that juvenile delinquency, as a social phenomenon, is socially constructed. More precisely, he wanted to show how the police, the judge, and the courts, but also the researchers themselves, transform the youths' actions into documents, texts, and written reports, which are then used as evidence to characterize certain acts or activities as being delinquent, illegal, dangerous, or suspicious. Cicourel examined the inquiries of police, educators, and judges because their inquiries, with their contingent features, establish the social classifications that designate and enable one to recognize the categories of deviance and conformity.

Cicourel (1968) first presented a number of statistics and questions their relevance to understanding crime, because the categories are inaccurate, ambiguous, or heterogeneous. They are ad hoc categories, far from the notions of precision and lucidity usually associated with the idea of the work of justice. Some of them are even rather curious, such as, for instance, the categories of fights between teenagers, or runaways. As Cicourel put it, these categories and the numbers associated with them have a "negotiable character" although they have a " 'solid' appearing nature." Cicourel then showed the structure of juvenile justice in the form of its verbal representations by educators and the adolescents and their parents. He then presented several cases of delinquency that he encountered during his research. I will present two.

In the first case, Audrey, a 15-year-old black girl, has committed several petty thefts from her classmates. She belongs to a middle-class family and lives in a tidy house, but her parents do not control her activities, the police say. In addition, she has had sexual intercourse "with at least two boys," the police say, who add that she is "a very appealing and attractive girl, . . . friendly, . . . not antisocial or psychotic." Although she often steals, Audrey does not behave as the usual chronic thief. Her look, her physical appearance, her behavior—her absence of insolence, for instance—cannot be used as "documents" to explain her thefts. Thus she is a candidate for clinical interpretations. A psychiatric report suggests that she is "emotionally disturbed." She is sent for observation to a psychiatric hospital for 90 days. Having thus been labeled, her future behaviors will always be interpreted in regard to this label by the police or social workers. It is cited in the case of an insignificant fight at school in which she took part to defend one of her friends. Every incident, however minor, is used to confirm the social and psychological initial diagnosis, and the categorization of each incident in turn builds up Audrey's delinquent identity.

Cicourel (1968) showed in other cases how delinquency cases are negotiated during the court trials. The destiny of the teenager depends on a large number of factors, such as the description of the case made by the police, the attitude of parents and that of the youth, and the presence or absence of an attorney.

In the second case, Linda is 13 years old. One evening, her mother takes her to a party that has been organized by her school for Christmas. Linda, however, does not actually go to the party; instead, she leaves with three boys and gets back home 2 days later. Her parents, who are worried about her being gone, call the police. Linda has left the school with the three boys, has been drunk on the whiskey stolen by one of the boys, has had sexual intercourse with them, and has not come back home because she was too drunk. The case is described by the police as being "juicy"; the detailed report runs several pages. The juvenile police, Cicourel says, have been very interested in Linda's sexual activities. One of the boys, Robert, who is 13, is seen as being the organizer of the encounter. His school behavior had caused him to be labeled as a potential delinquent. In school, he is considered to be a hopeless case.

Robert has been involved in 15 school "incidents," such as "smoking," "continuously chatting," "leaving class without permission," "interrupting other classes," "showing his friends a switchblade knife," and "having a continued defiance." The police report casts him as the only boy having had intercourse with Linda. In fact, the boys describe her as "a little whore who only thinks about sex." But the police report describes Linda as a pretty girl, polite, whose dress, hairstyle, voice intonation, and demeanor designate her as belonging to the middle class. She gives the impression of being "a nice girl."

The case is made more complex when, 2 months later, Linda's father arrives at the police station and declares that Linda has not come back home since the day before, when she went to a party where there was a lot of alcohol. When Linda's parents, accompanied by the police, arrive at the address, 30 to 40 boys and girls run away. Inside, Linda, who is drunk, is getting dressed, and she declares that she has just made love with 10 boys, among them Robert. The police report indicates, according to Linda's declarations, that all the boys pretended that they were Robert. For the boys of her school, Linda had become, since the previous incident, an "easy girl." They only had to make her drink.

The judge, during her questioning, asks Linda about her school performances, her school marks, her first sexual intercourse, her religious feelings, and so on. All this information documents the inquirer's opinion. Linda is very cooperative in the inquiry, she answers "well" to the questions, she seems to feel guilty. She says that she regrets what she has done, she will not do it again "until she gets married"; the boys have a wrong opinion of her, she says. She protests because now the whole school regards her as a "whore," because Robert has told everyone that she had completely undressed and then let them do "their own way." She was not so much denying the act she had committed, Cicourel notes, as worrying about her reputation. The interview shows us that the inquirer has an a priori favorable opinion of Linda. The questions she asks constitute a guide so that Linda can give the "good" answers, which show her will to reform, to make her "accidental" behaviors be forgotten: "Do you think God forgives you? . . . So, you think it was wrong? . . . Will you wait until you get married? . . . Will you change then?" The inquirer seeks also in the parents', and even in the grandparents', lives factors of stability and instability that could be related to Linda's conduct. In later interviews, Linda declares that her father gives her alcoholic drinks at home and has asked her to describe in detail her sexual experiences with the boys. Thus the father starts to be suspected of being responsible for what happens to Linda. He is, it is said, very keen on psychology; he has reputedly even once hypnotized Linda. She undergoes various psychological tests. The two investigators working on the case agree to recommend to the court that Linda should be sent to a psychiatric hospital for 3 to 6 months, with intensive therapy, and then should go home. The interviews with Linda and her parents are more numerous, but also with the juvenile judge and with Linda's teachers. The first report of the inquirers tended to criminalize the case. Then the elements about the father progressively made a psychiatric case of Linda. The dialogue occurring during the trial shows that the judge uses, in the file, elements that have already been judged during the interviews that informed the case. The parents accepted the court decision: Linda was sent to a psychiatric hospital, where she spent a month before coming back home. Because no charge was pending against her anymore, she was no longer under probation. Three months later, Linda failed to go back home again after a party.

According to Cicourel, these cases reveal, among other things, how the process of judicial inquiry is dealt with and negotiated. Police officers and judges, like any members of society, do their jobs with "background expectancies and norms of the social structure," which enable them to decide what is normal and what is not, to distinguish a "good guy" from a "hooligan," to define "defiance to authority" or what a "good family" is:

> The "delinquent" is an emergent product, transformed over time according to a sequence of encounters, oral and written reports, prospective readings, retrospective readings of "what happened," and the practical circumstances of "settling" matters in everyday agency business. (Cicourel, 1968, p. 333)

Contrary to what seem to indicate the police activity and the judicial statistics, the delinquents are not natural social types that can be encountered. Delinquency is the result of a social negotiation.

Laboratory Life

Ethnomethodology considers that social facts are produced, but people "forget" the practical activities by which they have produced them. Garfinkel and two of his students, Lynch and Livingston, applied these insights to scientific activity (Garfinkel et al., 1981).

The question of "making science" had already been treated before. The ethnomethodological approach reorients the problems studied in the sociology of science, which had been interested, for instance, in the influence of social factors on scientific discoveries and products. The ethnomethodologists' studies of science do not aim at showing how the social structures act on the scientific activity. They are interested in the scientific activity itself.

Garfinkel and his collaborators described the discovery of the optical pulsar made by four American astrophysicists on January 16, 1969. They analyzed three data sources: a recording of the conversations between the researchers during the night of their discovery, their notebooks, and the publication in a specialized journal of an article giving an account of their results. Garfinkel and his collaborators asked this question: What does the discovery of an optical pulsar consist of? They used a "Gestaltist" metaphor to explain it:

> Their discovery and their science consists of astronomically "extracting an animal from the foliage." The "foliage" is the local historicity of their embodied shop practices. The "animal" is that local historicity done, recognized, and understood as a competent methodic procedure. . . . Their science consists of the optically discovered pulsar as the procedured practical observability of their ordinary night's work. (Garfinkel et al., 1981, p. 132)

It is obvious, in the recorded conversations as well as in their notes, but not in the scientific article, that the result is obtained only during a series of historicized observations done in an actual length of time and in a precise order. During Observations 18, 19, and 20, they had to focus the telescope's objective, adjust the diaphragm size, start the computer program, and check the information given by the oscilloscope so that the pulsation of a star could be recorded during Observations 21, 22, and 23. The pulsation then stops, as the work goes on to a 37th observation. That is precisely the object of their work: We can perceive it through a series of gestures, words, deductions, doubts, uncertainties, or in a state of mental excitement. The scientific work is indeed the object of a localized construction.

To a stranger, their work of discovery appears to be a whole set of competent, analyzable practices. Their discovery consists of extracting a "cultural object": the pulsar. But it does not mean, Garfinkel et al. insisted, that this object, the pulsar, is an account; it makes the discovery work accountable: "The pulsar is not to be found in the words, but it cannot be found without them. The pulsar is attached to nature, not the account" (Garfinkel et al., 1981, p. 142). For Garfinkel et al., astronomy, in that it is a "discovering science" of objects of the real world, remains a science of practical action.

For ethnomethodology, the question raised by the sociology of science is therefore no longer to evaluate the sociocultural influences on the researchers, nor to know whether science is a social activity like any other. The aim of ethnomethodology in the scientific field is more ambitious. It seeks to demonstrate that the scientists use, in their research, a certain number of resources that they consider as natural (theories, logical reasoning, and results of past experiments), whose objectified character they forget, and which they no longer relate to the practical laboratory activity that has constructed them. The scientific work can only be transmitted because of this reification, as any scientific article on discoveries can show.

This field of research on science, opened by ethnomethodology, appears to be extremely fruitful and promising. It can, doubtlessly, lead to concrete applications. If we succeed in analyzing the activities through which the researchers find their fundamental results, we are entitled to think that this new understanding can result in greater scientific productivity. In the field of applied sciences and techniques, one can also guess what the object of an ethnomethodological work could be, if we bear in mind a certain number of catastrophes, more or less recent, in which human errors have been detected: nuclear (Three Mile Island and Chernobyl); maritime (oil slicks, North Sea ferry-boat or Black Sea cruiser accidents); airline (Tenerife, Washington, Madrid plane crashes, among others); and ecological (major chemical pollutions: Bhopal, Seveso, etc.). In this field as well as in others, ethnomethodological research could have implications for training and consequences of prevention.

Bureaucracy

The modern theory of bureaucracy began with Max Weber. But, according to Bittner (1965/1974),

[Weber] failed to explore the underlying common-sense presuppositions of his theory. He failed to grasp that the meaning and warrant of the inventory of the properties of bureaucracy are inextricably embedded in what Alfred Schütz called the attitudes of everyday life and in socially sanctioned common-sense typifications. (p. 74)

It is not enough, to prove one's birth date, to write it down on a piece of paper, especially if this proof is necessary for the constitution of an administrative file such as one that is required to obtain financial aid, a scholarship, or a pension. It is usually necessary to give a more reliable proof of one's age, when age is a condition of eligibility. As Zimmerman (1969/1974) emphasized, the administration bases its action on objective proof. But what gives a piece of paper official validity? How do its agents attribute to a document sufficient value as proof, and conversely, on what basis do they reject another one, whose content is seemingly identical?

In studying the working processes and the arguments used by a social work agency in a large city in the western United States, Zimmerman noted that for the employees of the agency, the documents often have an obvious character. For them, they are naturally relevant to establish the validity of, for instance, an application form. However, in spite of an existing, precise list of compulsory documents to provide, there are always staff-applicant negotiations entailed in judging the validity of an application form. There is a reciprocal interaction between the routines and the deviations, between the "obvious," unquestioned use of administrative documents and the endless incidents that make this use observable as part of rational processes. The obvious character of a document depends in fact on the representations that agents and applicants have of the world. Recognizing the obvious character of a document is the sign of the agent's professional competence. When a document is problematic, it is then the occasion of an analysis of the rules and procedures by which the decisions, either refusal or acceptance, are made.

In another publication concerning the same fieldwork, Zimmerman (1970) analyzed the practical application of the rules that agents in charge of information have to follow to direct the public in the various services of the social work agency. They have to judge the problem to efficiently direct people in their transactions. The agents use a whole set of routine rules to do their work. They have to make choices in "commonsense situations." The competent use of a particular rule to solve the problem in a "normal" way is based on the agent's understanding of the case. This use, which is the agent's special working knowledge, is based on experience and on a capacity to apply the rules, adjust the rules, or even make up ad hoc rules that permit him or her to treat the cases correctly. This possibility of deviation, and deviation when it occurs, is not the sign of a transgression from the rules but proof of the agent's competence and of a capacity to judge the situation and produce "reasonable" solutions, in light of the rules and of the problem posed.

7. CRITIQUES AND CONVERGENCES

The radical character of ethnomethodology did not fail to bring hostile response from established sociology. As Pharo (1984) wrote:

> By insisting that "the professional sociological inquiries are practical through and through" [Garfinkel, 1967/1984, p. viii], ethnomethodology stands from the start in a delicate position. . . . It is as if, by claiming that sociological reasoning, lay or professional, are formally identical, this identity being in their common character of practical accomplishments, ethnomethodology was sawing the branch on which sociology was seated. (p. 145)

In other words, in the field of sociology, *Studies* was taken as a declaration of war. The questioning of sociology had never been so radical. The war started as early as 1968, with the well-known review of *Studies* by James Coleman (1968) in *American Sociological Review*. Its climax was in 1975, with Lewis Coser's attack, in front of the American Sociological Association.

The Charge

In August 1975, Coser, who was then president of the powerful American Sociological Association, made a violent attack on what he regarded as the two main currents endangering American sociology: quantitative analysis and ethnomethodology.

In his opening address to the annual conference of the association, Coser (1975) said he is

> perturbed about present developments in American sociology which seem to foster the growth of both narrow, routine activities, and of sect-like, esoteric ruminations. . . . These two trends are an expression of crisis and fatigue within the discipline and its theoretical underpinnings. (p. 691)

In brief, his criticisms of quantitative sociology included a concern for its sophistication and a concern for the fact that its modern credo is based on regression and path analysis, which even regards the other quantitative methods as being obsolete. The weakness of the concepts and of the theoretical notions cannot be compensated for by measurement, however precise. He views the use of these methods as abusive, often guided by the desire of a fast career. Then he attacked ethnomethodology:

> It seems aggressively and programmatically devoid of theoretical content of sociological relevance. Limiting itself by a self-denying ordinance to the concrete observation of communicative codes, subjective categorizations, and conversational gestures, it underplays the behavioral aspects of goal directed social interaction. . . . Ignoring institutional factors in general, and the centrality of power in social interaction in particular, it is restricted to the descriptive tracing of the ways in which both individual actors and students of their activities account for their actions. . . . In some versions of ethnomethodology, inter-subjectivity is consciously neglected so that one ends up with a view of individual actors as monads without windows enclosed in their private and unshareable universes of meaning. (Coser, 1975, p. 696)

Coser (1975) reproached ethnomethodology for never having sought to be accepted by sociology, and for, on the contrary, deliberately limiting "its appeal to a few zealots, united in the belief that they possess a particular perspicacity, evidently denied to the others" (p. 696).

It is well known that ethnomethodology's esoteric language was said to function to delimit borders and alienate nonmembers. Such language

> can successfully camouflage relatively trivial ideas. . . . Another characteristic with obvious functional value that ethnomethodologists share with similar close groupings in other scholarly areas, is the characteristic habit to limit their footnote references almost exclusively to members of the in-group or to non-sociologists. . . . There is, in addition, a peculiar propensity to refer to as yet unpublished manuscripts, to lecture notes and research notebooks. (Coser, 1975, p. 697)

These last features make the ethnomethodological school appear like a sect rather than a field:

> Sects are typically closed systems, usually led by charismatic leaders and their immediate followers. They attempt to reduce communication with the outside world to a minimum while engaging in highly intense interactions between the True Believers. (Coser, 1975, p. 697)

Coser (1975) drew his arguments from the differences between Garfinkel, Sacks, Blum, and Cicourel to demonstrate that there is a sectarian organization: Some admit "the existence of rules and non varying processes which transcend the situations, others deny the possibility of analyzing a situation which is not specific" (p. 698). In short, there is a great variety of sources and of points of view among the ethnomethodologists, but they are all "idealists."

The "triviality" of the problems ethnomethodology is interested in is striking, Coser said. For instance, Sudnow (1972) wondered how to cross a street without being run over, which led him to develop a "sociology of a glance." Schegloff (1968) spent an important part of his investigations establishing the way our telephone conversations start and end. Some excellent studies, such as those of Bittner (1967) and Cicourel (1968), do not compensate for

> the enormous ballyhoo surrounding ethnomethodology . . . which amounts to an orgy of subjectivism, a self-indulgent enterprise in which perpetual methodological analysis and self-analysis leads [sic] to infinite regress, where the discovery of the ineffable qualities of the mind of analyst and analysand and their private construction of reality serves to obscure the tangible qualities of the world "out there.". . . By attempting to describe the manifest content of people's experience, ethnomethodologists neglect that central area of sociological analysis which deals with latent structures. (Coser, 1975, p. 698)

Coser concluded that we have to be careful "not to learn more and more on less and less."

The terms used by Coser in his attack were particularly severe for ethnomethodology. The following year, the whole set of his remarks brought a sharp debate among American sociologists, not only with ethnomethodologists but also with quantitativists, for whom Coser's address had created a commotion.

A Misinterpretation

In his answer published the following year, Zimmerman (1976) found unconvincing, and even confused, Coser's argumentation on the "crisis of the discipline." According to Zimmerman, Coser's hint at works about the sociology of science is more formal than guided by a genuine concern for research. He limits the notion of measurement to statistical techniques and does not provide any serious reason to believe that American sociology is in a crisis.

Coser devoted an important part of his address to insisting that ethnomethodology is a sect, aiming at pointing out its role in the waning of the discipline, Zimmerman wrote. This attack is founded on truncated quotations taken out of their context. Furthermore, Coser "is an example of the mistake made by a lot of commentators on ethnomethodology, who mistake the problem studied with its frame of occurrence" (Zimmerman, 1976). For instance, in his study of Agnes, Garfinkel had been reproached with being interested in a case of transsexuality rather than in the question of decision making in the hospital. Coser used the same processes to discredit Sudnow's article on the interactions between drivers and pedestrians, aiming at showing that both parties, "at a glance," decode the situation to determine their conduct. The condensation produced by the extraction of one or two sentences out of their context makes the reader believe that Sudnow, and thus ethnomethodology, are indeed interested in trivial objects, such as "glances." Coser transposed it, Zimmerman (1976) noted, "to the advice parents give to their children to be careful when crossing the street." This is how Coser tried to show the "triviality" of ethnomethodological preoccupations. He "made a caricature, by selecting two rather specialized examples among a great variety of ethnomethodological studies." This is why accusations of triviality in ethnomethodological studies are suspect. In fact, according to Zimmerman, Coser had not understood ethnomethodology. For instance, he had not understood the distinction between the content of a social interaction, as it can be seen by the participants or the observer, and the form of this interaction, which can be perceived clearly only if we replace our interest in what people do with a focus on how they do it. This is what Zimmerman called the "ethnomethodological reduction."

The "subjectivism" that so agitates Coser seems to be understood as an exclusive concern for what is in the mind of the member, where description of such contents constitutes the prime task. Moreover, the implication is that ethnomethodology treats such descriptions as definitive of social reality, that is, members' formulations of their circumstances are accorded a privileged status (Zimmerman, 1976, p. 9).

Coser failed to grasp a central tenet of ethnomethodology, not appreciating that members' formulations are not given a privileged exemption, nor are they conceived . . . as descriptions *of* or propositions *about* some domain. (That *members* conceive of formulations as being formulations *of* or *about* some field of events is quite another matter.) From our point of view, formulations are constituent features of the settings in which they are done. (Zimmerman & Pollner, 1970, p. 102)

This answer by Zimmerman (1976) is essential for a better understanding of ethnomethodology, which

treats members' accounts of the social world as situated accomplishments, not as informants' inside view of what is "really happening." Ethnomethodology's concern, in general, is the elucidation of how accounts or descriptions of an event, a relationship, or a thing are produced in interaction in such a way that they achieve some situated methodological status, e.g., as factual or fanciful, objective or subjective, etc. (p. 10)

A Sect?

As has been seen, Coser maintained that ethnomethodology was a sect because of the existence of charismatic leaders, an esoteric language uniting its followers, its ignorance of the sociological community, and its splitting into factions. But the history of Western intellectual thought, Mehan and Wood (1976) answered, is a long sequence of groups behaving like sects. Ethnomethodology is an intellectual movement that, like the others, was being known only by a few and has eventually been known by a larger public.

In spite of its so-called language esotericism, it has produced, during the past few years, several essays that have made its works known. The institutionalization of ethnomethodological ideas is now well advanced, contrary to Coser's allegations concerning their so-called confidential aspect.

As for the splits, they are in fact currents that have developed within ethnomethodology. They are not signs of weakness but, on the contrary, of growing diversity and strength. If the crisis of sociology is real, its source is not in ethnomethodology. The crisis comes from inside and is provoked by the conformity that Coser wished to impose on sociology.

Ethnomethodology is interested in the same phenomena as sociology but with a different perspective:

Sociology studies social structures. Social structures are treated as "objective and constraining social facts.". . . Ethnomethodologists claim that the objective and constraining social structures of the world are constituted by "social structuring activities" (variously called "practices," "methods," "procedures," "reality work"). . . . Ethnomethodologists study the social structuring activities that assemble social structures. (Mehan & Wood, 1976, p. 14)

This conception has its origin in phenomenology, more exactly in Garfinkel's reading of Husserl, Schütz, and Gurwitsch. These phenomenologists regarded the world of daily life as an assembling of "mental acts of consciousness." Garfinkel (1967/1984) transformed these mental acts into public, interactive activities: "The objective reality of social facts [is treated as] an ongoing accomplishment of the concerted activities of daily life" (p. vii). Social activities, in that they are interactions, constitute social facts, which do not exist independently of the practices that constitute them.

Ethnomethodologists have analyzed the processes by which researchers in the social sciences collect information in daily life or in official statistics, which they change into data by coding practices, then transforming these objectified data into a correlation matrix.

These works show that research in the social sciences is a social construction. Researchers decide the truth of something by having discussions together and by arguing. An organized consensus decides the truth of scientific knowledge: "In social sciences, the truth is not revealed, it is argued," said Zimmerman.

Coser (1975) said that ethnomethodology tends to ignore the "real world" in its research. But for him, the real world is the realm of "socio-economic groups, of political mechanisms, of the functions and dysfunctions of the manifest and the hidden," independent of the daily actions of concrete persons. These concepts grasp only a part of social life. Ethnomethodology seeks to give more significance to these notions by trying to understand how such notions as "political power" and "institutional factors" are connected in daily life.

Contrary to what Coser affirmed, the notion of constitutive practice does not reduce the problem of the social order to psychology. Ethnomethodology, through its analysis of human activities, seeks to study the social phenomena incorporated in our discourses and in our actions.

Ethnomethodology cannot be reduced to the phenomenological reduction. In fact, various methods, including laboratory experiments,
ethnographies and field studies, surveys, and video are all used with
extreme rigor.

Coser insisted that ethnomethodology does not bring new light to
sociology. In fact, Mehan and Wood responded that if some of us have
turned to ethnomethodology, it is precisely because traditional sociology does not say much about the social practices that it claims to give
an account of. Ethnomethodology can succeed in explaining them by
revealing the practices that structure daily life, including "oppression,
dogmatism, and absolutism." Knowing how social structures operate in
daily life enables actors to change them.

Conclusively, Coser's sociology is somewhat obsolete, being founded,
as it is, on the belief that natural science methods are best adapted for
the study of social facts. Traditional sociology was developed at the
time of triumphant positivism. It has to be renewed to adjust to a new
image of serious research, which appeared with such philosophers as
Sartre, Merleau-Ponty, Heidegger, and Wittgenstein.

An Attempt at a Synthesis

Pierre Bourdieu (1990) appeared to take both poles of contemporary
sociology into consideration. He wanted to go beyond the criticism
made of ethnomethodology, but keep at a distance with a fundamental
critique. In a lecture given at the University of California, San Diego,
in March 1986, Bourdieu went over a number of fundamental questions
for sociology and explained his theoretical choices. If he had to characterize his work in a few words, to apply a label to it, he would talk of
"constructivist structuralism" or "structuralist constructivism":

> By structuralism or structuralist, I mean that there exist, in the social world
> itself, and not merely in symbolic systems, language, myth, etc., objective
> structures which are independent of the consciousness and desires of agents
> and are capable of guiding or constraining their practices or their repre-
> sentations. By constructivism, I mean that there is a social genesis, on one
> hand of the patterns of perception, thought and action which are constitu-
> tive of what I call the habitus, and on the other hand of social structures,
> and in particular of what I call fields and groups, especially of what are
> usually called social classes. (1990, p. 123)

Social science, Bourdieu (1990) wrote, oscillates between two apparently incompatible positions, objectivism and subjectivism:

> On the one hand, it can "treat the social phenomena as things," in accordance with how the old Durkheimian maxim has it, and thus leave out everything that they owe to the fact that they are objects of cognition—or of miscognition—in the social existence. On the other hand, it can reduce the social world to the representations that agents make of it, the task of the social science then consisting in producing an "account of the accounts" by the social subjects. (p. 124)

It is in the works of Schütz and of ethnomethodologists that Bourdieu saws "the purest expressions of the subjectivist vision." According to him, the problem in this vision is the fact that scientific knowledge is "in continuity with the common sense knowledge, since it is only a construction of constructions," whereas objectivism is characterized by "a break with primary representations."

Bourdieu meant to go beyond this opposition between objectivism and subjectivism, which he regards as artificial. He wrote:

> I could sum up in one phrase the whole analysis I am setting out for you today: on one hand, the objective structures which the sociologist constructs in the objectivist moment, by setting aside the subjective representations of the agents, are the basis of the subjective representations and they constitute the structural constraints which influence interactions; but, on the other hand, these representations also have to be remembered if one wants to account above all for the daily individual and collective struggles which aim at transforming or preserving these structures. This means that the two moments, objectivist and subjectivist, stand in a dialectical relation and that, even if for instance the subjectivist moment seems very close, when it is taken separately, to interactionist or ethnomethodological analyses, it is separated from them by a radical difference: the points of view are apprehended as such and related to the positions in the structure of the corresponding agents. (Bourdieu, 1990, pp. 125-126)

We must question Bourdieu's analysis, which reduces ethnomethodology to a subjectivist stance. Ethnomethodologists have shown that commonsense reasoning and scientific reasoning have a common basis, and even have identical processes, but this does not mean that ethnomethodology confuses lay knowledge of the social world by ordinary people and the scientific knowledge that sociologists construct of this lay knowledge. The sociologist necessarily does a task of objectivation to transform empirical objects into sociological objects, and the ordinary member of society does similar work by interpreting his surrounding world as he conducts his daily interactions, but the latter does not have the same interest as the sociologist in analyzing this process. Bourdieu does not appreciate that ethnomethodology emphasizes that lay and professional constructions of the social world are both practical, and not subjective, activities. The opposition between Garfinkel and Bourdieu is founded on a difference in their conceptions of practice, a difference that is represented by their respective notions of member and habitus. We already have seen that for Garfinkel, being a member does not refer to social status but implies the mastery of the natural language of a given social group, and more generally, the tacit mastery of its ethnomethods. For Bourdieu, habitus, which is at the heart of the reproduction of social classes, comprises the overall character of an individual or a social class; he writes of whole "schemes generating social stratification and practices," "similar to genetic capital," that produce coherent action but whose significance in doing so escapes the consciousness of the social actor.

Marxism and Ethnomethodology

One could expect a more violent antagonism between Marxism and ethnomethodology. In fact, attempts to bring them closer exist from both sides. Mehan and Wood (1975) devoted several pages to this question. Zimmerman (1978) concluded his article with the same perspective. Chua (1977) noted important convergence points: According to him, ethnomethodology can be considered as a practice of demystification and of "de-objectivation" of the reified categories of "the natural attitude." It brings to light reality as a social accomplishment in the contemporary capitalistic society.

However, according to Jean-Marie Brohm (1986), the social relationships seem to be reduced, for ethnomethodology, to

a swarming of individual practical initiatives, an assembling of conscious, free, and autonomous actions of agents who have the possibility of choosing between multiple alternatives or linguistic or pragmatic variances.

. . . The very notions of structure and of social relationship seem totally absent from the ethnomethodological approach. (p. 8)

In fact, there is a common basis to the works of Marx and Garfinkel. The convergence is double: On one hand, it concerns the permanent construction of society by itself; on the other hand, it implies the reification of this construction and the transformation, in a Sartrian language, of the works of practical activity into a pratico-inerte world.

In other respects, Sartre (1976), in a passage of his *Critique of Dialectical Reason*, criticized the "fetishism of totality" in Kurt Lewin. Sartre wrote that Lewin forgot the production of the group as a totality that seems to be natural and finished, as a unified organism. But, contrary to the organism that is the model of structural-functionalism, there is never group totality but always a totalization in process. This phenomenological analysis by Sartre is very close to what Garfinkel wrote at the same period.

Cornelius Castoriadis (1965/1987), writing from both a Marxist and a phenomenological orientation, opposed the "instituting society" and the "instituted society." Quéré (1986) has proposed a debate between this orientation and ethnomethodology, indicating that the latter also has the "work of institution" as an object, although it does not use the term.

In opposition to traditional sociology, which sees institutions as the constraining frame of our practices, ethnomethodology insists on focusing on the ordinary instituting process of daily life as the construction of the institution. Ethnomethodology takes the institution, not as a reified and stable entity, but as an active process of institution.

CONCLUSION

On September 30, 1987, at a conference held in Paris,[6] Garfinkel gave a lecture titled "The Strange Seriousness of Professional Sociology." This lecture celebrated the 50th anniversary of Parsons's book, *The Structure of Social Action*. In that lecture, which coincided with the 20th anniversary of the publication of his *Studies*, Garfinkel reminded his audience that ethnomethodology was born from a rereading of Durkheim's aphorism, saying that "the objective reality of social facts is sociology's fundamental principle."

In Paris, Garfinkel reiterated the famous definition that is in the very first lines of the preface to *Studies*, a key formula that gives the most direct and deepest access to the ethnomethodological project:

> The objective reality of social facts, in that every society is locally produced, naturally organized, reflexively accountable, ongoing practical achievement, in that this objective reality being everywhere, always, only, exactly, and entirely members' work, is sociology's fundamental phenomenon.

The significance of this slogan, Garfinkel concluded, is to point to a new set of research instructions. The formula must be used in concrete fieldwork.

This is what Garfinkel emphasized in the last part of his lecture in Paris. He reminded his audience that 20 years after the publication of *Studies*, "there is a large corpus of empirical studies of practical actions." He mentioned some of the ethnomethodological works that explore the range of the field of sociology and that demonstrate that the social order is "locally and interactionally produced, naturally organized, and reflexively accountable." These studies, Garfinkel said, have revealed phenomena whose existence was not even suspected. They are radically distinct from classical sociological studies in that they insist on the production and the accountability of social order. Only ethnomethodological studies are able to show how members of a society "produce and exhibit together, in their ordinary life, the coherence, the strength, the ordering character, the meaning, the reason and the methods of social order."

NOTES

1. This book was first published in French: A. Coulon, 1987, *L'ethnométhodologie*. Paris: Presses Universitaires de France (3rd ed., 1993, Que sais-je? No. 2393). I am very grateful to Jack Katz, Professor of Sociology at the University of California, Los Angeles, and to Terri L. Anderson, a graduate student at UCLA, for assistance in preparing the English version of this book.

2. I have begun to edit a new periodical in France, the first issue of which appeared in June 1993: *Cahiers de Recherche Ethnométhodologique*, Laboratoire de Recherche Ethnométhodologique, University of Paris VIII.

3. The users of the Parisian metro may question the innumerable declarations of politicians, taken up with insistence by the media, about the rise of delinquency in the Parisian metro at the end of the 1980s. How are the crime statistics made, and by whom? By the metro company agents, by policemen, by judges? Has not our point of view changed, on certain crimes that have existed for a long time but that were not counted as such? Do the statistics refer to the same categories of crime? Are not the controls more numerous? Are they thefts, muggings, or simply the fact that someone is traveling without a ticket? To answer these questions, it is necessary to make inquiries about the inquiries.

4. This notion of participant observation—common in the sociological tradition—is to be related to the notion of "unique adequacy" proposed by Garfinkel. It indicates that the researcher has to become familiar with the milieu on which he or she is doing research.

5. The research team included Hugh Mehan, Robert McKay, Marshall Shumsky, Kenneth Leiter, David Roth, and Kenneth and Sybillin Jennings, all students of Cicourel. With this research work, conducted between 1968 and 1969, they wrote their dissertation theses, which were later submitted at the University of California, Santa Barbara.

6. This conference, jointly organized by the CNRS and the CNET, was titled "Analysis of Action and Analysis of Conversation." It was held at the Maison des Sciences de l'Homme in Paris, September 28-30, 1987.

REFERENCES

Bachmann, C., Lindenfeld, J., & Simonin, J. (1981). *Langage et communications sociale* [Language and social communications]. Paris: Hatier.

Bar Hillel, Y. (1954, April). Indexical expressions. *Mind, 63*(250), 359-387.

Becker, H. (1963). *Outsiders: Studies in the sociology of deviance.* New York: Free Press.

Bellman, B. (1975). *Village of curers and assassins.* The Hague, Netherlands: Mouton.

Bellman, B. (1984). *The language of secrecy.* New Brunswick, NJ: Rutgers University Press.

Benson, D., & Hughes, J. (1983). *The perspective of ethnomethodology.* London: Longman.

Berger, P., & Luckmann, T. (1966). *The social construction of reality.* Garden City, NY: Doubleday.

Bittner, E. (1963). Radicalism: A study of the sociology of knowledge. *American Sociological Review, 28,* 928-940.

Bittner, E. (1967). The police on skid-row. *American Sociological Review, 32,* 699-715.

Bittner, E. (1974). The concept of organization. In R. Turner (Ed.), *Ethnomethodology* (pp. 69-81). Harmondsworth: Penguin. (Original work published 1965)

Blumer, H. (1969). *Symbolic interactionism: Perspective and method.* Englewood Cliffs, NJ: Prentice Hall.

Boden, D., & Zimmerman, D. H. (Eds.). (1991). *Talk and social structure.* Cambridge, UK: Polity Press.

Bourdieu, P. (1990). *In other words. Essays towards a reflexive sociology.* Stanford, CA: Stanford University Press.

Brohm, J. -M. (1986). L'ethnométhodologie en débat [The ethnomethodological debate]. *Quel corps? 32-33,* 2-9.

Castaneda, C. (1968). *The teaching of Don Juan.* Berkeley: University of California Press.

Castaneda, C. (1972a). *Journey to Ixtlan.* New York: Simon & Schuster.

Castaneda, C. (1972b). *Sorcery: A description of the world.* Unpublished doctoral dissertation, University of California, Los Angeles.

Castoriadis, C. (1987). *The imaginary institution of society.* Cambridge, UK: Polity Press. (Original work published 1965)

Chua, B. H. (1977). Delineating a Marxist interest in ethnomethodology. *American Sociologist, 12,* 24-32.

Cicourel, A. (1964). *Method and measurement in sociology.* New York: Free Press.

Cicourel, A. (1968). *The social organization of juvenile justice.* New York: John Wiley.

Cicourel, A. (1970). The acquisition of social structure: Toward a developmental sociology of language and meaning. In J. D. Douglas (Ed.), *Understanding everyday life* (pp. 136-168). London: Routledge & Kegan Paul.

Cicourel, A. (1972). *Cognitive sociology: Language and meaning in social interaction.* New York: Free Press.

Cicourel, A., Jennings, K., Jennings, S., Leiter, K., McKay, R., Mehan, H., Roth, D., & Shumsky, M. (1974). *Language use and school performance.* New York: Academic Press.

Cicourel A., & Kitsuse, J. (1963). *The educational decision-makers.* Indianapolis, IN: Bobbs-Merrill.

Coleman, J. (1968). Review symposium on H. Garfinkel's *Studies in ethnomethodology*. *American Journal of Sociology, 33*, 122-130.

Conein, B. (1987). Les actions politiques sont accomplies localement et temporellement [Political action is accomplished locally and processually]. *Raison présente, 82*, 59-63.

Coser, L. (1975, December). Presidential address: Two methods in search of a substance. *American Sociological Review, 40*(6), 691-700.

Coulon, A. (1990). *Le métier d'étudiant: Approches institutionnelle et ethnométhodologique de l'entrée dans la vie universitaire* [The student's craft: Institutional and ethnomethodological perspectives on the entrance to university life]. Unpublished doctoral dissertation, University of Paris VIII.

Coulon, A. (1993). *Ethnométhodologie et éducation* [Ethnomethodology and education]. Paris: Presses Universitaires de France.

Coulon, A. (1994). *L'école de Chicago* [The Chicago school] (2nd ed.). Paris: Presses Universitaires de France.

Drew, P., & Heritage, J. (Eds.). (1992). *Talk at work. Social interaction in institutional settings*. Cambridge, UK: Cambridge University Press.

Emerson, R. (1969). *Judging delinquents*. Chicago: Aldine.

Erickson, F. (1975). Gatekeeping and the melting pot: Interaction in counseling encounters. *Harvard Educational Review, 45*(1), 44-70.

Flynn, P. (1991). *The ethnomethodological movement: Semiotic interpretations*. Berlin and New York: Mouton de Gruyter.

Gabel, J. (1975). *False consciousness: An essay on reification*. Oxford: Blackwell.

Garfinkel, H. (1949). Research note on inter- and intra-racial homicides. *Social Forces, 27*, 370-381.

Garfinkel, H. (1952, June). *The perception of the other: A study in social order*. Unpublished doctoral dissertation, Harvard University, Cambridge, MA.

Garfinkel, H. (1956). Conditions of successful degradations ceremonies. *American Journal of Sociology, 61*, 420-424.

Garfinkel, H. (1959). Aspects of the problem of common sense knowledge of social structures. *Transactions of the Fourth World Congress of Sociology, 4*, 51-65.

Garfinkel, H. (1963). A conception of, and experiments with, "trust" as a condition of stable concerted actions. In O. J. Harvey (Ed.), *Motivation and social interaction, cognitive determinants* (pp. 187-238). New York: Ronald Press.

Garfinkel, H. (1984). *Studies in ethnomethodology*. Cambridge, UK: Polity Press. (Original work published 1967, Englewood Cliffs, NJ: Prentice Hall)

Garfinkel, H., Lynch, M., & Livingston, E. (1981). The work of a discovering science construed with materials from the optically discovered pulsar. *Philosophy of the Social Sciences, 11*, 131-158.

Garfinkel, H., & Sacks, H. (1970). On formal structures of practical action. In J. C. McKinney & E. A. Tiryakian (Eds.), *Theoretical sociology* (pp. 338-366). New York: Appleton-Century-Crofts.

Giglioli, P. P., & Dal Lago, A. (1983). *Etnometodologia* [Ethnomethodology]. Bologna: Il Molino.

Heritage, J. (1984). *Garfinkel and ethnomethodology*. Cambridge, UK: Polity Press.

Herpin, N. (1973). *Les sociologues américains et le siècle* [American sociologists and the century]. Paris: Presses Universitaires de France.

Hilbert, R. A. (1992). *The classical roots of ethnomethodology: Durkheim, Weber, and Garfinkel.* Chapel Hill: University of North Carolina Press.

Hill, R. J., & Crittenden, C. S. (Eds.). (1968). *Proceedings of the Purdue Symposium on Ethnomethodology* (Institute Monograph Series, No. 1). West Lafayette, IN: Purdue University, Institute for the Study of Social Change. (Review symposium appeared in *American Sociological Review, 33*)

Jules-Rosette, B. (1975). *African apostles: Ritual and conversion in the church of John Maranke.* Ithaca, NY: Cornell University Press.

Jules-Rosette, B. (1985, September). Entretien avec Harold Garfinkel [Interview with Harold Garfinkel]. *Sociétés, 5*(1), 35-39.

Katz, J. (1988). *Seductions of crime: The moral and sensual attractions of doing evil.* New York: Basic Books.

Latour, B., & Woolgar, S. (1979). *Laboratory life: The social construction of scientific facts.* Beverly Hills, CA: Sage.

Livingston, E. (1978). *An ethnomethodological investigation of the foundations of mathematics.* Unpublished doctoral dissertation, University of California, Los Angeles.

Lynch, M. (1979). *Talk in a research laboratory.* Unpublished doctoral dissertation, University of California, Irvine.

MacIver, R. M. (1942). *Social causation.* Boston: Ginn.

McHugh, P. (1968). *Defining the situation.* Indianapolis, IN: Bobbs-Merrill.

Mehan, H. (1971). *Accomplishing understanding in educational settings.* Unpublished doctoral dissertation, University of California, Santa Barbara.

Mehan, H. (1978, February). Structuring school structure. *Harvard Educational Review, 48*(1), 32-64.

Mehan, H. (1979). *Learning lessons: Social organization in the classroom.* Cambridge, MA: Harvard University Press.

Mehan, H. (1980). The competent student. *Anthropology and Educational Quarterly, 11*(3), 131-152.

Mehan, H. (1982). Le constructivisme social en psychologie et en sociologie [Social constructivism in psychology and sociology]. *Sociologies et Sociétiés, 14*(2), 77-95.

Mehan, H., & Wood, H. (1975). *The reality of ethnomethodology.* New York: John Wiley.

Mehan, H., & Wood, H. (1976, February). De-secting ethnomethodology. *American Sociologist, 11*, 13-21.

Moerman, M. (1968). Accomplishing ethnicity. In R. Turner (Ed.), *Ethnomethodology* (pp. 54-68). Harmondsworth: Penguin.

Mullins, N. (1974). *Theories and theory groups in contemporary American sociology.* New York: Harper & Row.

Ogien, A. (1984). *Positivité de la pratique. L'intervention en psychiatrie comme argumentation* [Positivity of practice. Intervention in psychiatry as argumentation]. Unpublished doctoral dissertation, University of Paris VIII.

Ogien, A. (1989). *Le raisonnement psychiatrique* [Psychiatric reasoning]. Paris: Méridiens-Klincksieck.

Paperman, P. (1982). *Le travail: Routines et ruptures du sens commun* [Work: Routines and ruptures of common sense]. Unpublished doctoral dissertation, University of Paris VIII.

79

Park, R., & Burgess, E. (1921). *Introduction to the science of sociology.* Chicago: University of Chicago Press.

Parsons, T. (1937). *The structure of social action.* Glencoe, IL: Free Press.

Pharo, P. (1984). L'ethnométhodologie et la question de l'interprétation [Ethnomethodology and the question of interpretation]. In *Arguments ethnométhodologiques. Problèmes d'épistémologie en sciences sociales* (Vol. 3, pp. 145-169). Paris: CEMS-EHESS.

Pharo, P. (1985). La description des structures formelles de l'activité sociale [The description of formal structures of social activity]. In *Décrire: Un impératif?* (Vol. 2, pp. 159-174). Paris: EHESS.

Pierrot, L. (1983). *Interactions sociales et procédures cognitives de production de sens. Le travail pour les femmes immigrées* [Social interactions and cognitive procedures in making sense. The work of immigrant women]. Unpublished doctoral dissertation, University of Provence, Aix-en-Provence.

Pollner, M. (1974). Sociological and common-sense models of the labelling process. In R. Turner (Ed.), *Ethnomethodology* (pp. 27-40). Harmondsworth: Penguin.

Psathas, G. (1980). Approaches to the study of the world of everyday life. *Human Studies, 3,* 3-17.

Psathas, G. (1995). *Conversation analysis: The study of talk-in-interaction.* Thousand Oaks, CA: Sage.

Quéré, L. (1984). L'argument sociologique de Garfinkel [Garfinkel's sociological argument]. In *Arguments ethnométhodologiques. Problemes d'épistémologie en sciences sociales* (Vol. 3, pp. 100-137). Paris: CEMS-EHESS.

Quéré, L. (1986). Comprendre l'ethnométhodologie [Understanding ethnomethodology]. *Pratiques de Formation, 11-12* 23-24, 29-37, 67-75.

Rosenbaum, J. (1976). *Making inequality.* New York: John Wiley.

Sacks, H. (1963). Sociological description. *Berkeley Journal of Sociology, 8,* 1-16.

Sacks, H. (1972). Notes on police assessment of moral character. In D. Sudnow (Ed.), *Studies in interaction* (pp. 280-293). New York: Free Press.

Sacks, H. (1992). *Lectures on conversation* (Vols. 1-2). Oxford: Blackwell.

Sartre, J.-P. (1976). *Critique of dialectical reason, theory of practical ensembles.* Atlantic Highlands, NJ: Humanities Press.

Schegloff, E. (1968, December). Sequencing in conversational openings. *American Anthropologist, 70,* 1075-1095.

Schegloff, E. (1990). On the organization of sequences as a source of "coherence" in talk-in-interaction. In D. Dorval (Ed.), *Conversational organization and its development* (pp. 51-77). Norwood, NJ: Ablex.

Schütz, A. (1962). *Collected papers* (Vol. 1). The Hague, Netherlands: Martinus Nijhoff.

Schütz, A. (1972). *Der sinnhafte aufbau der socialen welt* [The phenomenology of the social world]. London: Heinemann. (Original work published 1932)

Sharrock, W., & Anderson, B. (1986). *The ethnomethodologists.* Chichester, UK: Ellis Horwood.

Shumsky, M. (1972). *Encounter groups: A forensic scene.* Unpublished doctoral dissertation, University of California, Santa Barbara.

Signorini, J. (1985). *De Garfinkel à la communauté électronique Géocub: Essai de méthodologie (et de recherche des fondements)* [From Garfinkel to the Geocub elec-

80

tronics community: A methodological essay]. Unpublished doctoral dissertation, University of Paris VII.

Sudnow, D. (1967). *Passing on: The social organization of dying.* Englewood Cliffs, NJ: Prentice Hall.

Sudnow, D. (Ed.). (1972). *Studies in social interaction.* New York: Free Press.

Thomas, W. I., & Znaniecki, F. (1927). *The Polish peasant in Europe and America.* New York: Alfred A. Knopf. (Original work published 1918-1920, University of Chicago Press)

Veron, E. (1973). Vers une logique naturelle des mondes sociaux [Toward a natural logic of social worlds]. *Communications, 20,* 246-278.

Widmer, J. (1986). *Langage et action sociale. Aspects philosophiques et sémiotiques du langage dans la perspective de l'ethnométhodologie* [Language and social action. Philosophic and semiotic aspects of language within the ethnomethodological perspective]. Unpublished doctoral dissertation, University of Fribourg, Switzerland.

Wieder, D. L. (1974a). *Language and social reality.* The Hague, Netherlands: Mouton.

Wieder, D. L. (1974b). Telling the code. In R. Turner (Ed.), *Ethnomethodology* (pp. 144-172). Harmondsworth: Penguin.

Wilson, T. P. (1970). Normative and interpretive paradigms in sociology. In J. D. Douglas (Ed.), *Understanding everyday life* (pp. 57-79). London: Routledge & Kegan Paul.

Wilson, T. P., & Zimmerman, D. H. (1979-1980). Ethnomethodology, sociology and theory. *Humboldt Journal of Social Relations, 7*(1), 52-88.

Zimmerman, D. H. (n.d.). *Fieldwork as a qualitative method.* Unpublished manuscript.

Zimmerman, D. H. (1970). The practicalities of rule use. In J. D. Douglas (Ed.), *Understanding everyday life* (pp. 221-238). London: Routledge & Kegan Paul.

Zimmerman, D. H. (1974). Fact as a practical accomplishment. In R. Turner (Ed.), *Ethnomethodology* (pp. 128-143). Harmondsworth: Penguin. (Original work published 1969)

Zimmerman, D. H. (1976, February). A reply to Professor Coser. *American Sociologist, 11,* 4-13.

Zimmerman, D. H. (1978). Ethnomethodology. *American Sociologist, 13,* 6-15.

Zimmerman, D. H. (1987, June). Sequential and institutional contexts in calls for help. *Social Psychology Quarterly, 50*(2), 172-185.

Zimmerman, D. H., & Pollner, M. (1970). The everyday world as a phenomenon. In J. D. Douglas (Ed.), *Understanding everyday life* (pp. 80-103). London: Routledge & Kegan Paul.

Zimmerman, D. H., & Wieder, D. L. (1970). Ethnomethodology and the problem of order: Comment on Denzin. In J. D. Douglas (Ed.), *Understanding everyday life* (pp. 285-295). London: Routledge & Kegan Paul.

Additional References

Button, G. (1991). *Ethnomethodology and the human sciences.* Cambridge, UK: Cambridge University Press.

Douglas, J. (Ed.). (1971). *Understanding everyday life.* London: Routledge & Kegan Paul.

Mead, G. H. (1934). *Mind, self and society from the standpoint of a social behaviorist.* Chicago: University of Chicago Press.

Mehan, H., Hertweck, A., & Meihls, J. L. (1986). *Handicapping the handicapped.* Stanford, CA: Stanford University Press.

Pollner, M. (1987). *Mundane reason: Reality in everyday and sociological discourse.* Cambridge, UK: Cambridge University Press.

ABOUT THE AUTHOR

ALAIN COULON is currently Professor in the Education Department at the University of Paris VIII at Saint-Denis and Dean of the Faculty of Education, Communication, and Psychoanalysis.

His fields of interest are education and sociology, especially ethnomethodological and interactionist approaches. Over the past few years, he has been working on how freshmen survive at the university and how they learn their jobs of being students through a process of what he has defined as *affiliation*. He has also conducted research on the teaching of library work.

He is the author of *L'Ecole de Chicago* (1994) and *Ethnométhodologie et Éducation* (1993). He is also the editor of *Cahiers de Recherche Ethnométhodologique*, published by the Laboratory for Ethnomethodological Research, of which he is the director, at the University of Paris VIII at Saint-Denis.

Printed in the United States
97882LV00002B/25/A